CW00408263

An Angler's Journal

A lifetime's fishing
told in 52 tales

*with pages to record
your own angling adventures*

John Tomsett
illustrated by Marvin Huggins

First published 2020
by John Catt Educational Ltd,
15 Riduna Park, Station Road,
Melton, Woodbridge IP12 1QT
Tel: +44 (0) 1394 389850
Email: enquiries@johncatt.com
Website: www.johncatt.com

ISBN: 978 1 913622 32 9

Testimonials for *An Angler's Journal*

When the sliver of silver handed to your future wife is a small chub, when your four-year-old's first fishing trip turns into a "carnival of chaos", *An Angler's Journal* is as much a delightful reflection on landmarks in life's meandering journey as it is a chronicle of memorable catches during half a century at the butt of a rod.

Each expedition, retold with photographic clarity, is about much more than an elusive trout, a recalcitrant pike or a coy carp.

Each trip, is a staging post, a window for thrill yet also for quiet reflection – a rare combination that angling provides. Amusing, evocative, emotional, fin-sharp in its descriptive recollections, *An Angler's Journal* brings beautiful sense to man's enduring fascination with the sport of fishing.

**Andy Dunn, Chief Sports Writer,
Daily and Sunday Mirror**

Like an angling T. S. Eliot, John Tomsett has measured out his life with fishing rods. In this evocative, moving and funny memoir, Tomsett offers 52 riverside reveries, delicately casting his words to capture the elusive essence of this most reflective of pastimes. *An Angler's Journal* isn't just about fishing, though there are plenty of beautifully-described encounters with pike, perch and trout; it's a book about friendship, family and finding meaning through a lifetime's obsession with "the fish landed and the fish lost.

**Simon Bainbridge, Professor in English and Creative Writing,
University of Lancaster**

———

An Angler's Journal is so much more than a fisherman's diary. Here are bright, burning memories of moments of exhilaration and despair that all anglers will recognise. Whether he is telling tales of his early angling apprenticeship – teasing tench from lazy Sussex lakes in the sun-kissed summers of the seventies, or regaling us with the challenge of chasing late-season sea trout on his beloved Yorkshire Esk – Tomsett's story-telling is captivating.

His writing elegantly chronicles the rich rewards that a lifetime of angling has afforded him. Through his love of angling have come timeless friendships and indelible family memories. Most importantly perhaps, angling has given him the time to "have stood still for the joy of it all"; *An Angler's Journal* is Tomsett's gentle invitation for us to do the same.

Dave Smith, former Primary Headteacher and member of the Yorkshire Fly-Fishers' Club

John Tomsett's *An Angler's Journal* is a wonderfully crafted collection of short tales documenting one man's lifetime of fishing escapades that fellow anglers will enjoy and relate to in equal measure. From the moment I opened the cover, I vowed I would use this wonderfully illustrated book to keep a record of my angling adventures in the years to come!

Steve Guppy, former Leicester and England footballer and avid angler

———

For Tom,
who has taught me more
than he has ever realised
on our fishing trips…

About the Authors

John Tomsett has been an angler his whole life. He grew up in Sussex. As a youth he was an outstanding amateur golfer but chose a career in the school classroom rather than on the golf course. Currently, fishing on the Yorkshire Esk provides him an escape from the pressure of his day job as a state secondary headteacher in York.

Marvin Huggins is a self-taught artist based in York. He specialises in oil and pencil, although he works in a wide-range of media. In 2015 he was made a Member of the Guild of Aviation Artists when a number of his works were exhibited at London's Mall Gallery. Whilst he has painted and drawn subjects ranging from motorsports to animal portraits, this is his first venture into angling art. instagram.com/marvs.artwork

Retrieving the past

"In the past, nothing is irretrievably lost, but rather, on the contrary, everything is irrevocably stored and treasured."

Viktor E. Frankl

This is a book for you, the reading angler, to help ensure you do not make the same mistake I made, many years ago, when I failed to keep an angling journal.

In these pages, you will find 52 tales from my angling life – symbolically, one for every week of the year – beautifully illustrated by my close friend and artist, Marvin Huggins.

In writing these tales, I have had to work incredibly hard to retrieve from my memory the detail of myriad fishing trips, some from over half a century ago. Despite Frankl's claims to the contrary, for every tale recalled I am sure there is another lost forever in the unkempt corners of my mind. And even these 52 are *tales*, with all the story-telling liberty that label granted me, as my memory failed.

Frankl might have been right when he wrote that everything in our past is "stored", but a memory can only be "treasured" if you know where to find it. By keeping the briefest records in this journal, you'll be able to retrieve more easily from your memory store the details of your favourite angling adventures over the coming months and years: the fish landed and the fish lost; the sunrises and the sunsets…*the sheer thrill of going fishing.*

"Tight lines", as they say –

John Tomsett, September 2020

Apprentice

Abbey's Lake was a young boy's delight. It is where I learnt to fish. Deep in the remnants of the Sussex Weald forest, its nearest village, Maresfield, was famous for its role in iron production for centuries. In the streams and paths that wound through the surrounding woods, you could find literally tons of iron ore waste with its shiny, crazed surface of greys and purples.

If you walked beyond Abbey's and its Powder Mill House, towards Piltdown through Park Wood, you crossed Batt's Bridge stream. The narrowing of this rivulet through the small culvert's tunnel transformed this brook into a decent sized pool, with a strong central current and substantial eddies. It was crouching at the edge of this pool that my angling career began. That afternoon in the late 1960s, I can remember as a five year old watching my dad stalk a chub for nearly an hour before he caught it. He was a study in patient persistence.

Dad was born a few miles away, at Sharpsbridge. He had fished the Sussex Ouse, just yards from his house, his entire childhood. His olive skin and affinity for the natural world were born on the banks of that river. So, coaxing a chub from the large pool on Batt's Bridge stream should have been no trouble at all.

All he had was a six-foot yellow fibreglass rod with a green, fixed centre-pin reel. It was a cheap piece of kit. The grayling-style float was bright red above and bare cork below. Three BB. Size 8 hook. And, fresh from our manure pile at the bottom of the garden, a brandling worm. I watched as dad baited up in front of my nose and the worm emitted a yellow liquid as it squirmed apoplectically.

I looked on, the apprentice to the expert. Dad flung the tackle out into the current at the head of the pool. The float flipped up and settled. It slowed naturally. He held the rod tip as high as he could to keep the line off the surface of the water. It glided into the near eddy, shook and then slid away at speed. *Strike!* He missed. His hook came up wormless. The water was so clear he could see the fish take the bait. He then spent the next forty-odd minutes varying his approach, to no effect. Fishless, he came up the bank, put down the rod, took out a penknife and said, "Come on. I've got an idea."

I followed him as he scoured the forest floor. He found a decent twig, six inches long, whittled it down and two rubber float caps later it was floating through the pool with a new brandling suspended six feet below. A minute more, we had a 6oz chub on the bank. To me it was a silver leviathan.

And from that moment on, I was always going to be an angler.

An Angling Adventure to Remember

Venue:

Day: Date: Time:

Water conditions:

Weather conditions:

Catch details:

Fishing method:

Specimen details:

Notes:

An Angling Adventure to Remember

Venue:

Day: Date: Time:

Water conditions:

Weather conditions:

Catch details:

Fishing method:

Specimen details:

Notes:

Progress

I was fortunate that my formative fishing years were largely spent on Abbey's Lake. Its well-kept, lily-padded swims, tree-lined banks and dam wall afforded anglers like me a wide variety of fishing opportunities. There were two routes to Abbey's that brought you out on opposite sides of the water. One way took you through dense woods; the other across wide meadows. A deep, extensive reed bed at the mouth of the lake made it impossible to walk its entire circumference.

The first swim you came to via the meadow route was peg 33, high up in the reeds. It was a swim that shrank as summer progressed and the lily pads grew back after the annual pre-season clearance. It was the place for the very best anglers to catch the carp that basked there. The next notable swim was not a peg at all. Five or six huge trees leant from the bank with their branches' tips brushing the water ten yards out into the lake. They created a contained pool, which was regularly full of perch. You could lean on a trunk and watch the fish circle round before hoiking a few out with a quill float and a lobworm on a size 10 hook.

The dam end of the lake was the place to catch tench and perch, and fishing in the waterfall pool often gave up a decent trout. Peg number 9, otherwise known as *Big Bay*, was the most popular and its neighbour was a fine spot to catch large, golden-scaled rudd. Fish anywhere from peg 9 along to peg 1 and you'd be sure to find roach and tench aplenty.

Abbey's was a wilderness to be explored. It was unspoilt, the *Maresfield Angling Club's* measured maintenance programme ensured that the lake's thirty-odd pegs did not compromise its natural appearance. Just back from the waterfall sat the Mill House where Cecil Deadman lived, a shadowy figure who died when the building burnt to the ground over three decades ago. In its stead stands a modern mansion. I only know this after a sentimental visit to Sussex a couple of years ago. Instead of Abbey's' largely unkempt banks, I found manicured lawns, acre after acre of them. Where once was impenetrable undergrowth, park benches allowed residents fine views across the water. It was utterly unrecognisable, to the point where I wondered for a second whether I had taken a wrong turning. But no, this was my once beloved Abbey's, my angling playground, denuded of all its natural charm.

Further research revealed it had been redeveloped as an up-market "corporate bookings only" fly-fishing and clay shooting venue. A public path runs exactly where it used to 40 years ago – much to the annoyance of the private owners, I'm sure – but that is where public access ends. One certainty in life is that nothing remains the same, but some changes hurt more than others.

First

When you're young, four years between brothers is a big age gap. When my elder brother Dave began secondary school, I was only halfway through primary. That difference makes him *much* older. Whilst I was still having milk at break time, he was being tempted for a fag behind the groundsman's hut at the secondary modern, two miles down the road.

On the insistence of mum and dad, I used to tag along with him to everything: around the golf course; up the village's recreation field playing football with his older mates; off picking potatoes for the farmer; to Abbey's, fishing.

Angling is largely a social activity when you are young. Groups of lads go fishing all day and it becomes the major event of a weekend. What it allowed me to do was to see my brother with his older mates, and watch how he behaved out of view of our parents. It was both illuminating and exciting. We had moved from Parklands, the big council estate at the north end of the village, to a similar dwelling in a row of six at the south end. It meant he had to try harder to be included.

I used to watch whilst Dave and his pals smoked, swore, larked around and sometimes caught decent fish. If one of them landed a tench it was a big deal. None of them, for all their secondary school bravado, really wanted to handle the slimy creature. But I learnt what to do and what not to do from watching them. To a seven year old it was an education, on many levels.

In order to stay out of the way, I would keep a low, but observant, profile and, with a jam pot and net, catch fry from the water's edge. The glittery wonders kept me amused. I was obsessed with them and always felt disappointed when they expired in front of my admiring eyes.

In time, I was allowed to use our all-in-one fibreglass yellow rod and green reel to fish, with a big red cork float and the smallest hook my brother could find in the tackle box. The centre pin reel meant casting was nigh on impossible. I had to strip the line off then cast. The more line I stripped off, the further I could get out but the more chance there was of a bird's nest.

Constantly entangled, I spent all day fishing six feet out for the same fry I had been trapping in my jam jar, until, remarkably, I reeled in to find a rudd had taken my bait and was dangling, in all its 2oz glory, right there in front of my eyes. I went home unbearably excited. It was a tale to be told to anyone who would listen…and it still is.

An Angling Adventure to Remember

Venue:

Day: Date: Time:

Water conditions:

Weather conditions:

Catch details:

Fishing method:

Specimen details:

Notes:

An Angling Adventure to Remember

Venue:

Day: Date: Time:

Water conditions:

Weather conditions:

Catch details:

Fishing method:

Specimen details:

Notes:

Risk Assessment

There are certain odd moments from being in Year 2 at primary school that I can still recall, like reading aloud at the front of the class and saying *soldier* instead of *shoulder* and the whole class laughing at my mistake. And the time when I spent the entire morning, undetected by our teacher, Mrs Humphreys, on my hands and knees beneath the tables, only to find, when I emerged from my *subtablean* excursions, that my brand new trousers had holes in both knees. *Oh, how I cried!*

What I remember most clearly, however, was being allowed to go off across the fields and down through the woods to check our lay-lines. The stream at the bottom of the hill beneath the school was so narrow it was, with a decent run-up, jumpable. It was home to a plethora of small trout, none more than a pound in weight. They were, however, tricky to catch as the water ran clear and they could see you at 100 feet. If it coloured a little after rain it was possible to hook a good few, but once the stream turned mud-brown fishing was pointless.

So, most of the time it was nigh impossible to catch the trout. Stalking our prey was way beyond the skills of a bunch of excited six year olds. We were hopeless hunters. The solution was a lay-line. Lay-lines are illegal. They are, essentially, baited up, unsupervised fishing lines. To make one you fashion a sturdy but slim, six to eight inch wooden stake from a tree branch. You then cut a 30 foot length of line and tie it to the wooden stake. At the non-stake end, you tie a hook, baited with a juicy lob worm. The stake is fixed securely into the base of the riverbank, well-hidden from view.

The line is cast out into the pool and left overnight to lure an unsuspecting trout.

Mrs Humphreys once allowed me and my mate Wrakey to leave the class at break time, run down to the end of the field, climb the school fence, traverse the steep, brackened bank, crawl under the electrified barbed wire, walk through the bluebell wood, leap the river, sprint up to the Nursery Lane pool through a field of cows, check our lay-line (which was, predictably, troutless, as we had, on that occasion, for some unfathomable reason, used red string, rather than fishing line), cross the road at the Underhill bridge and amble back again.

We could have been drowned, electrocuted, drowned, trampled by a herd of cows, drowned, knocked down by a car, poisoned (if we had eaten the toxic toadstools), and, finally, if nothing else had done for us, drowned. And we were unaccompanied. Yes, *unaccompanied*, alone, teacher-less and most definitely without a parental permission letter. Those *really were* the days...

Peg 1

The best spot to fish on Abbey's Lake was peg 1. It was at the very top end of the water. A barely discernible path through jungle-like undergrowth brought you to a perilously thin boardwalk, at the end of which was a narrow platform, reserved for the bravest anglers.

The lake's biggest carp and tench were caught from peg 1; on match days it was the peg everyone wanted to draw. As a ten year old I'd always walk past peg 1, as if it were haunted. I wouldn't even look down the overgrown path as I made for *Big Bay* from which beginners like me could fish, safe in the knowledge that falling in was highly unlikely.

On 10 July 1974, however, everything changed. A sunny day had settled into a cloudless, still evening. When I emerged alone from the wooded path and the tree canopy lightened as the lake came into view, for some reason I turned left. I decided that, for the first time ever, I would fish peg 1.

I dumped my kit and navigated my way out onto the platform. Peg 1 was a gorgeous gap amongst the lily pads. On the left, beyond the pads, the lake disappeared into a wall of tall bulrushes. I stood on the platform and looked down into the water. It was churned and muddied, alive with feeding fish. Swathes of fine bubbles dotted the surface. I tackled up, my trembling fingers barely able to thread the line through the guides. I had a Mitchell 324 reel, a brown 12 foot rod from Woolworth's, a 3 BB onion float and a size 8 hook tied direct to 4lb Maxima line. I didn't really know what I was doing, but a chunk of bread flake fished just off the bottom did the trick.

The float wavered in the water and rose an inch. I struck. I hooked into what felt like Moby Dick's big brother. It lunged for the safety of the weed beds. Downwards it drove. I hung on. Somehow, so did the hook. Several minutes later a tench's deep green flank was visible.

My landing net was a cheap, short-handled game fishing affair, the only one dad could afford. I had managed to leave that at the wrong end of the boardwalk. I wedged the rod butt into the platform's wooden slats and made a run for it. I returned with the net to find, miraculously, the rod still there and a tight line. I pointed the rod skywards, leant over and netted my first ever tench, all 3lb 6oz of it. I went on to catch another, a few ounces lighter.

In Mr Ashman's Year 5 class the following Monday, during diary-writing hour, I wrote endlessly about peg 1 and the fish I'd caught on the "Tench of July".

An Angling Adventure to Remember

Venue:

Day: Date: Time:

Water conditions:

Weather conditions:

Catch details:

Fishing method:

Specimen details:

Notes:

An Angling Adventure to Remember

Venue:

Day: Date: Time:

Water conditions:

Weather conditions:

Catch details:

Fishing method:

Specimen details:

Notes:

Elementary Education

In an ideal world, it will rain buckets on a Tuesday and Wednesday. The Esk will spate on Wednesday evening, up to two metres higher than normal. The fish will start moving up from Whitby on a Thursday and by 5 am on a September Saturday the sea trout and salmon will be several miles inland on stretches of the river near Glaisdale. With any luck, 48 hours of swimming into the current will make them foolhardy and ravenous.

These days a river-cam allows anglers to assess the levels of rainfall and the depth of the river without having to leave home, which is handy as it is a 120 mile round trip for me. Never great to travel that far and find the water unfishable: either gin clear or chocolate brown. The peak moment to fish is when the river runs tea-like and two or three feet higher than usual. That is when you seek out the sandy riverbeds above rapids or a waterfall, where the fish rest up after their exertions.

I did not realise until I reflected upon my obsession with river levels in North East England, that I had learned that sensory perception as a young child in rural Sussex. At primary, if it rained the chatter in the playground was all about what the stream would look like after school and who was off fishing.

It did not take much for the leapable stream at the bottom of our field to turn unfishably mud-coloured. A decent spell of rain in the morning would be enough to give the stream sufficient colour to allow a pack of novice anglers to fish without scaring the trout. Once school was over, the scramble home to get our kit would culminate in meeting at the road bridge on Underhill and us leap-frogging each other pool-by-pool as we worked our way down a two-mile stretch. Too much water and we would traipse back home before a line was cast, too little and we would try our luck in case the river coloured up before our eyes.

If the rain had been just right, we would be out all evening, catching wild brown trout of up to a pound in weight. It was where we acquired the essential rudiments of fishing. We were semi-skilled apprentices, learning by doing, trial and error. A rain-dependent angling education that has lasted a lifetime.

Obsession

It had been a preternaturally hot summer's day in 1976. Late June and early July that year saw the temperature rise above 30°c repeatedly. Abbey's sweltered in the gruelling sun. The scorching air sat heavily on the surface of the lake. Blue-green dragonflies balanced upon the bulrushes, seemingly too tired to fly. The fish swam to the bottom, desperate for respite from the heat. Nothing stirred.

I had spent all afternoon traipsing round the lake, from empty swim to empty swim. I was a lone angler. I'd spun for perch down at the dam end of the lake; I had float-fished for rudd in the lilies on peg 11 and legered for tench on the corner of the waterfall. As afternoon lazed slowly into evening, the temperature began to drop. The slightest breeze rippled up, and then fell a moment later.

I had been at the lake for over nine hours and not seen a soul. I hadn't seen a fish, either. With an hour of daylight left, tops, I considered calling it a day. I felt wary of walking through the dense woods in the dark so took the meadow route home, past peg 33, where the carp often lolled around in the far reed bed. You could stand at the top of the bank on the edge of the field, and see right across the peg. There, at the end of the pool, in a ten foot gap in the lily pads were several carp. The water was so clear, I could see they were all commons. They were just hanging in the water. If they moved at all, it was imperceptible. The sun had stunned them into statues.

A particular specimen caught my attention; it was the closest in, but I was not sure I could land my bait anywhere near it. With my heaviest onion float, I hurled my rig at the fish. One time I cast so hard I launched myself off the platform and into the water. Undeterred, I cast and recast but the carp stayed resolutely beyond my reach at the end of the swim amongst the lily pads. Once or twice it shifted itself a few inches further away when my top cast disturbed it, but it was a lost cause from the start. Time had all but stopped as I fixated on my elusive quarry. I was consumed by the moment.

By the time I awoke from my obsession with this fish, it was nearly dark. A barn owl rose and swooped across the water. After *five* last casts, I scooped up my creel, scrambled up the bank and set off. I arrived back home well after 11 pm. It was the only time ever that I found my dad waiting for me at the top of the path outside our house.

An Angling Adventure to Remember

Venue:

Day: Date: Time:

Water conditions:

Weather conditions:

Catch details:

Fishing method:

Specimen details:

Notes:

An Angling Adventure to Remember

Venue:

Day: Date: Time:

Water conditions:

Weather conditions:

Catch details:

Fishing method:

Specimen details:

Notes:

Lord of the Flies

What motivates us to fish? Well, I don't dedicate a whole journal entry to the time I caught a couple of gudgeon. Many of my life's angling highlights involve catching a big fish or when the fishing itself has been perilous or amusing. It is surely the need to deceive another animal and exert our control over it that, somehow, drives the angler. That instinct is deeply ingrained in the human psyche. In *Lord of the Flies*, novelist Wiliam Golding explores how a group of boys, marooned on a desert island, grow increasingly barbaric. At one point, they kill a wild pig and Golding describes the satisfaction the boys take from the "knowledge that they had outwitted a living thing, imposed their will upon it, taken away its life like a long satisfying drink."

When you grow up in the countryside, you get to understand the darker side of the natural world. Out in the woods death and cruelty abound. And you learn how to control your own brutal instincts.

In Yorkshire they use the term "laiking about". The word "laik" derives from the Viking word for "play", and having been one myself and having two of my own, I know all about the shenanigans young lads can get involved in when they are out laiking.

Shortbridge stream is about 20 miles inland from Newhaven, where the Sussex Ouse enters the English Channel. For a male sea trout to make the upper reaches of the stream for the spawning season is a miracle of endurance and navigation no human will ever entirely comprehend. To be met at the end of that journey by a bunch of stupid lads who are both fascinated and frightened by you, is an undeserved fate for such a magnificent creature.

We spotted the exhausted fish whilst out laiking one late autumn Saturday afternoon. What really sticks out in my memory of that day, nearly 50 years ago, was the trout's "kype", or hook jaw. We all thought it was a salmon. We chased it up and down a shallow stretch of the stream. It was totally exhausted and hardly had the energy to evade the missiles we threw at it.

Eventually, my mate waded in and, with the spike end of a bank stick, poked the fish around until it went belly up. He dragged the poor thing out and held it up in triumph. It was my *Lord of the Flies* moment, at first thrilling and then repulsive. It taught me the hollow futility of asserting one's authority over a living thing that is without the facility to resist.

I knew from that day forth that we must treat the fish we catch with the greatest respect and handle them like precious ornaments. It was a lesson learned that has stayed with me throughout my angling life.

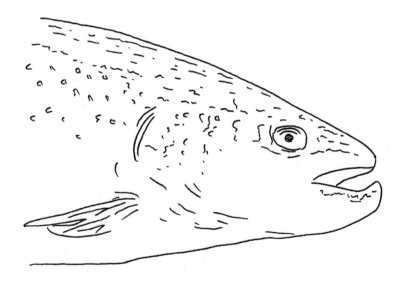

Too Many to Handle

Tench are known as the *Doctor Fish*. Legend has it that poorly fish rub against a tench because tench slime has healing properties. In his poem "Gutteral Muse" my favourite poet Seamus Heaney sits at his hotel window late on a summer's night feeling like "an old pike, all badged with sores", aching to be young again amongst the young men and women from the discotheque whose voices float up to him from the car park like tench bubbles.

My formative years as an angler were spent catching tench. By ten years old, I was a competent angler. I had learnt a lot from fishing with Jim Cyster, one of my brother's mates, as well as accumulating knowledge of what did and didn't work through spending hours just *fishing*.

One day Jim and I were down at Abbey's Lake and we set ourselves up at peg number 9, *Big Bay*. There was so much space that three or four people could fish it with ease. Whilst it was accommodating, it was rarely productive. But that overcast, damp day we really couldn't stop catching fish. We got set up with bubbles appearing on the surface everywhere. They were best bubbles too – the fine ones that come up in a rush, a sign that several feet below there is a tench burrowing in the bed of the lake for food.

We fished bread flake on size 8 Mustad hooks tied direct to 4lb line. We would put all the shot just below the float, bar one BB which was placed four inches from the hook. The flake would lie on the bottom, along with the BB shot. It meant that we could detect lift bites easily. We were soon into fish. We caught tench after tench after tench. I had never been into a shoal of tench before nor have I since. I remember I even caught one just three inches long.

As the day progressed, we kept adding to the keep net. To Jim's growing irritation, I began hauling it up to look at the fish. A net full of tench was a thing of wonder to someone of my age. My dad came down to the lake on a walk, and I eagerly showed him our haul.

We must have had close to twenty fish in the net when I pulled it up yet again to have a peek. Just as it came clear of the water, and there was nothing to bear the weight of our haul but the lead which held the mesh together at the bottom, with a cataclysmic swoosh, the whole thing gave way. Instead of peering in and seeing the grumpy, red-eyed tench staring back at me, there was the lake and the wide open net where the fish had been. I'd lost the lot.

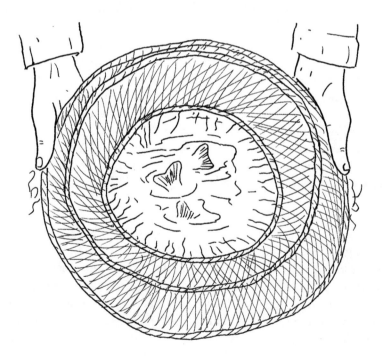

An Angling Adventure to Remember

Venue:

Day: Date: Time:

Water conditions:

Weather conditions:

Catch details:

Fishing method:

Specimen details:

Notes:

An Angling Adventure to Remember

Venue:

Day: Date: Time:

Water conditions:

Weather conditions:

Catch details:

Fishing method:

Specimen details:

Notes:

Worth the Irritation

I have a genuine soft spot for the diminutive crucian carp. This muscular powerhouse is relatively tiny compared to its gargantuan relatives, the common and the mirror carp. The British rod caught record is only 4lb 10oz. Yet, pound for pound it is one of the best fighting fish you could hope to hook.

Jim had discovered that hallowed of all things, the yet-to-be-fished, bang-in-the-middle-of-nowhere, farmyard pond. It was on the edge of a tiny East Sussex hamlet, Fives Ashes. Jim's dad knew the farmer who casually mentioned the pond's existence and off Jim and I traipsed at 5 am one August morning in the mid-1970s, to see what on earth we might catch.

The first time we went we saw nothing at all. No rises, no bites, no sign of fish. Our sole reward from that initial visit emerged the following day: a string of bites from an invisible insect predator. The thing was, the farmer had told Jim's dad that he had seen fish in the pond, so, undaunted by both blanking and bite bumps, we made a second foray to see what we might catch. It was one of those mornings that bodes well: mist on the water, a sunny day ahead. We had resolved to stay until dusk.

Jim was a meticulous fisherman. Where I was all *size 8 tied direct to 4lb Maxima*, he was much more *hook to nylon*. His kit was beautifully looked after and he fished with utter precision. And he was incredibly patient. Ten fishless hours after we had arrived at the farm, Jim went for a walk. He was crouching behind a huge bankside oak when he whistled, motioning for me to take a wide berth away from the water's edge to join him.

The farmer had been right. Underneath the overhanging branches were three plump looking fish, suspended there, a foot or so beneath the surface. We edged away. Jim returned minutes later. He gently lowered his float fished bread flake into the water. Nothing. He sat there for forty minutes, stock still, watching his float. I observed from a distance. Suddenly he struck. His light rod doubled over. I came running with the net but it was a while before we saw a fish at all.

Jim kept a tight line and his float moved just above the surface of the pool at an obstinately serene pace. His innate patience won through. He kept the pressure on the fish and the float rose imperceptibly higher above the water until a deep golden brown flank became visible. Eventually, there, on the bank was a perfectly formed crucian carp, weighing well over 2lbs. My reward came 12 hours later, when I woke up covered in insect bites.

Manor Pond

One of my clear memories of growing up was living with the fact that my dad had chronic angina. As a postman, dad's heart condition meant he was given his own post van and a single round through the country lanes of Palehouse Common, near Uckfield, the Sussex town where we lived. It took the pressure off him walking and having to carry a heavy bag of post. What it afforded him was the chance to forge strong, life-enriching relationships with the men and women to whom he delivered letters.

One of dad's friendships from which I benefitted directly was with Norman and Guy, the two housekeepers at *Arches Manor*, a gorgeous eight bedroom, 16th century mansion. Hugh Vaughan-Thomas, Glamorgan cricketer and brother of the BBC radio presenter Wynford, owned *Arches* but was rarely there. It was typical of such residences, in that it had a decent pond which, back in the day, would have provided the manor house's inhabitants with many a decent meal.

Norman and Guy loved my dad and allowed me to fish the carp pool whilst the three of them drank wine and danced to Dolly Parton singing "Stand By Your Man". When I first started, I was a bit rubbish at the fishing, thinking that the bigger the fish – and there were some monster carp in that pond – the bigger the bait required. The tennis balls of bread I used as bait were completely inconsumable.

One evening, Jim and his dad came along. Jim brought his specialist carp rod with him. Jim knew a thing or two about how to fish. Unable to tempt a carp, I had lost interest and been reduced to catching tiny roach and rudd on maggots. Jim had set up a leger rig just to my right. He had a sophisticated bite detection system – a red washing up bottle top between the first and second guide, which he kept tight to the ground with a twig lodged in the lawn. It was a thing of beauty, especially when it rattled hard against his rod. I turned round to see him strike and the carp rod bend more than I thought possible.

What happened next amazed us all. Instead of Jim engaging in a protracted battle with a double figure carp, this huge eel came tail-walking across the surface of the pond, straight at us, like an Arabian Knight's whirling scimitar. Jim reeled in frenziedly. The eel thumped into the bank below, span round, snapped the line and, before we knew it, vanished back into the mud of *Arches Manor* pond.

I spent the rest of the session, as darkness fell, sitting stock still, Ted Hughes-like, with the "hair frozen on my head" for what I might catch, for what might be staring up at me from the ancient depths.

An Angling Adventure to Remember

Venue:

Day: Date: Time:

Water conditions:

Weather conditions:

Catch details:

Fishing method:

Specimen details:

Notes:

An Angling Adventure to Remember

Venue:

Day: Date: Time:

Water conditions:

Weather conditions:

Catch details:

Fishing method:

Specimen details:

Notes:

Luck

Back in the 1970s, as long as you had an Environment Agency licence, anyone could fish Piltdown Pond at any time. Its worn banks were proof of how it was pummelled by anglers the first few weeks of the season. After that, it was pretty much a waste of time trying to tempt a fish from its water. Now it is one of the *Copthorne & District Angling Club*'s venues, whose members have lavished care upon it in recent years and it boasts some decent specimens, with big carp, and tench to 7lb.

As a kid, I only ever once caught a tench at Piltdown, and it was a weird affair. We'd gone night fishing, which was a particularly grim adventure at *Pilters*. I had just begun secondary school and we had carted a modest amount of kit down to the pond and set up on the bank by the road.

An all-nighter was always much colder than it promises to be, even on the closest of evenings. Night fishing was about the *craic* rather than the fish. It was about seeing who would turn up, the glow of the rashly smoked fags, the sudden fish-scaring stampede of lads to see some dead carp in the reeds, the sense that you were doing something just a little bit dangerous, slightly edgy.

Mother would always pack me off with sandwiches, but I would end up eating the bread I had brought for bait as my brother's older mates would snaffle my grub. With no tents, a dirty sleeping bag, and no ground sheet to ward away the damp, fishing all night at Piltdown was about survival. Catching fish was an irrelevance.

I was ham-fistedly legering, launching my basic rig as far out as I could, without any rod rests and certainly no bite indicator. Every so often I would reel in just to reset the bread flake and recast into the void. On one such occasion, I was reeling in when suddenly the rod tip began thumping. It was odd, like a fish had taken a spinner. I played out a 2lb tench.

But I knew things weren't right. It wasn't foul hooked, like I suspected. No, the fish had someone else's hook stuck in its lip and a short length of line coming out of its mouth. On the line were two BB shot tight next to each other. My hook had jammed between the two shot as I reeled in and stuck there, all the way into the landing net. For my hook to have caught up on the line as it did and then to have remained wedged between the shot as the fish fought, was mind-bogglingly lucky.

My tench was the night's highlight and made the dreadful, mid-morning walk home – beyond tired, limbs aching – just that bit more bearable.

Resilience

If you are a male PE teacher and your surname is Bates, there is a good chance that your life will be made intolerable by the clever dick lads. But *Mister* Bates at our school was an exception. I do not remember him ever getting any stick. He was a calm, wise man. He was disciplined, but fair. He still took classes but rarely got involved in a kick about. He had no cartilage left in his knees, which were just a mass of brutal scarring.

He was probably in his mid-forties, but, as teenagers, Batesy seemed ancient to us. It is likely that our genuine respect for him derived from the fact that he ran a fishing club. After school for the last five Wednesday evenings of the summer term, we used to bundle into the minibus like the *Bash Street Kids* and head off down the A26 to fish the Sussex Ouse somewhere between Lewes and Isfield. I observed the hassle it was to take half-a-dozen students fishing and, years later, recalled Batesy's calm demeanour when *I* was the teacher running my own school angling expeditions.

Every fishing club trip followed the same pattern: we would get set up, he would check we all had an operating rig with bait in the water, and then instruct us to bother the oldest student should we come to any grief. With that, he would settle down to four hours of uninterrupted angling. Repeatedly, each of us would get in a tangled mess and the poor sixth former's evening would descend into unpicking one bird's nest after another, whilst Batesy carried on fishing oblivious to our travails.

One particular session we were mooching about queuing up to have our lines unravelled, when someone suddenly said, "Batesy's in". I looked up and, sure enough, his 12 foot fibreglass quivertip rod was arched over. I wandered up to watch, my kit dumped by my creel. Within a minute, my fellow hapless anglers had followed suit.

We stood a respectable distance from our revered teacher. Not once did he look round. He carried on playing his fish. It was clearly huge. The rod tip did not lurch haphazardly; rather it remained bent double as this specimen fish moved steadily across the swim. He was fishing with incredibly light gear – 3lb line and a size 18 hook – and, consequently, had no desire to bully his quarry into the net.

After what seemed an age, a giant bream surfaced, completely spent. The vast, bronze, disc-shaped fish glided across the water towards the net. It must have been well into double-figures. And then, as if in slow-motion, the fish spewed the hook out and drifted away. Batesy swung in the rig, examined it, baited up and cast out again. He tightened the line, set the quiver, turned round and said, "What are you lot staring at?"

An Angling Adventure to Remember

Venue:

Day: Date: Time:

Water conditions:

Weather conditions:

Catch details:

Fishing method:

Specimen details:

Notes:

An Angling Adventure to Remember

Venue:

Day: Date: Time:

Water conditions:

Weather conditions:

Catch details:

Fishing method:

Specimen details:

Notes:

Striped Surprise

Sussex woodlands are home to many natural waters, none, perhaps, more tantalising in its piscine promise than Fairhazel pond. Hidden away between Uckfield and Piltdown, it is fed by a trickling ditch which runs into Shortbridge stream. Several decades before a new bypass opened up access to the pond, it was a well-kept secret.

For a handful of reasons few people fished it: one, because it was not well-known; two, it was pretty inaccessible; and three, it seemingly contained nothing more than thousands of tiny roach and rudd. Rumours circulated of a huge perch, but nothing verifiable and certainly no evidence of such a fish existed within my circle of teenage fishing mates.

As a youth there is something satisfying about catching a fish a cast. You know it's easy-pickings, but it's infinitely better than blanking. And subconsciously, you keep track of how many you catch, just so you can brag about it when you get to school.

One particular morning on Fairhazel I was nearing 100 fish – mostly rudd and roach, punctuated by the odd, equally diminutive, perch – when the waggler slid away again. I struck with a certain nonchalance, but was met by significant resistance. I lifted hard, thinking I had caught the bottom, only for the rod tip to thump twice in return as the waggler, hanging just above the surface, lurched swiftly to the right and disappeared under the water.

I hadn't, at that stage of my novice angling career, bothered with adjusting the drag on the reel. Fishing 2lb breaking strain line to a single maggot on a size 18 hook, I reversed reeled and let line out, whilst ensuring I kept a tight connection between me and whatever it was I had just hooked. I had to play this submerged monster cack-handedly, praying I would be able to land it with my short, entirely inappropriate, game fishing landing net.

A couple of minutes into the fray and right in front of me, about ten feet out, the fish surfaced. A large spiked dorsal fin emerged. It was one of the fabled Fairhazel perch, much mythologised, rarely seen. Though resigned to losing the fish on my frail kit, I kept calm and, much to my own amazement, played it out. As it swept in front of me, tiring and slightly aslant, I lunged with my stubby net and secured it first time.

A cavernous mouth, lethal spikes, deep green and black broadside, I held it timorously in the late June sunshine, stunned at its grandeur. I had scales and an old camera in my bag. I recorded it, both by weight and on film. The following week a shot of my 3lb 4oz striped surprise made the *Angling Times*.

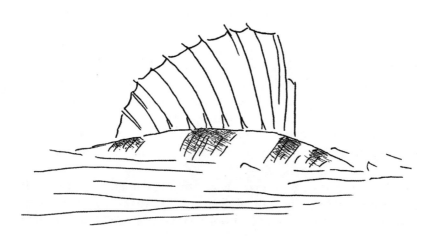

Two Loves Collide

I caught a 10lb common carp on floating bread crust at Horsted Place pond on Sunday 22 July 1984 at 6.10 pm with my mate Meade. It's not that I have an extraordinary memory, it's just that my other sporting love is golf, and on that date, at that time, my golfing hero Seve Ballesteros was busy winning the British Open at St Andrew's.

The pond was largely untouched and unfished. It was down in a valley at the bottom of a field, characterised by overhanging tree growth. The Uckfield Post Office had fishing rights and my postman dad gave me licence to fish for decent sized wild carp and tench.

A keen golfer, I usually spend the final day of the British Open laid flat out on the sofa watching the golf. That afternoon, however, Meade – a non-golfer – had turned up and fancied going fishing. We had just been through taking our A levels together. He is a good mate and, at that point, it looked like the American, Tom Watson, was going to win. So, off we went, with a crusty loaf, a sturdy rod and a size four hook. The only other bit of kit I took with me was a radio, so I could keep track of the golf. Despite the location, radio reception was remarkably clear.

So, there I was with Meade, eyes on the cruising carp, ears on the struggles of the golfing Spaniard. The fish were feeding off the top, as the early evening sun cast tree-shaped shadows across the water. A particularly large looking common, more gold than brown in colour, was hoovering up the loose crust I had scattered in the right hand corner of the pond. I watched whilst listening to events 500 miles north. Seve had a birdie putt on the 18th hole; Watson was in trouble on the 17th where he had shoved his approach shot out onto the road to the right of the green.

The carp sucked at the last piece of free crust. Just the hooked one remained. Meanwhile, Watson had dropped a shot. Good. Seve was back in with a chance. The carp nuzzled my crust. The commentator was all hushed tones. I listened on as he described Ballesteros lining up his putt on the last.

I shouted to Meade that Seve could now win. The voracious carp decided, just at that moment, that my crust was worth the gamble and tore off with it in its mouth. Seve's ball dropped and the crowd around the green cheered the Spaniard's famous matador celebrations.

I stood up, struck hard and was elated by both the golfing news and the fact that I had set the hook. The pond was weed free. It was merely a matter of wearing the fish down. Ten minutes later, Meade netted the carp and Seve was declared that year's Open Champion.

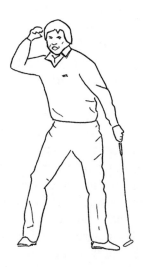

An Angling Adventure to Remember

Venue:

Day: Date: Time:

Water conditions:

Weather conditions:

Catch details:

Fishing method:

Specimen details:

Notes:

An Angling Adventure to Remember

Venue:

Day: Date: Time:

Water conditions:

Weather conditions:

Catch details:

Fishing method:

Specimen details:

Notes:

Romance

When your future wife comes to your Sussex home to meet your family for the first time and stays a few days, there are a number of things you might do: go out to eat; catch a film at the local cinema; go shopping into Brighton. But when your home town also boasts a decent river you might just take her float fishing bread flake for chub – if you're an angling obsessive and have zero emotional intelligence, that is.

My teenage years were spent in Uckfield, East Sussex, known best for it being the last place Lord Lucan, socialite and alleged wife-murderer, was seen alive. The River Uck occasionally features on the national news, when it breaks its banks and floods the local shops. It is the river where I learnt how to trot with an Avon float. It's also where I caught a number of notable fish over the years – some decent brown trout in a stretch through nearby Buxted Park, the odd nice perch and a number of good size chub.

It was an untouched river. Fishing just outside the town, heading west, you were quickly in the deepest countryside. The river flowed through one of the finest wild flower meadows, where you'd find, amongst a range of different grasses: cornflowers; poppies; buttercups; oxeye daisies; cow parsley; teasel; wild daffodils; foxgloves; honeysuckle; and endless dandelions.

Crouching down in the riverbank amongst the flora and fauna of the Sussex countryside, trotting downstream at distance until the float shoots under – you have good connection with the hook because you have learnt how to feed the line effectively – and banging into a decent chub, was pretty good sport. Well, it was, until the industrial estate was built in the late 1980s. Tarmac replaced meadow.

To accommodate industrial units and a link road, the meandering river's haphazard course and its accompanying trees, which created huge corners, with eddies and currents for the different species of fish to inhabit, was straightened out. I had studied Larkin's poetry at university, and when the Uck was disfigured and the wild flower meadow was erased, the lines from his poem written for the Environment Agency, "Going, Going", never seemed more apposite: "It seems, just now,/ To be happening so very fast;/ Despite all the land left free/ For the first time I feel somehow/ That it isn't going to last."

Before the developers did their worst, however, I managed to persuade my girlfriend Louise to not only come fishing with me but agree that I could teach her the rudiments of trotting, to the point that, with dogged persistence, she caught a 6oz chub. I even made her hold the slimy thing. It was no big issue – she's a fully paid up northerner, after all. It might even have sealed the deal, considering she continues to tolerate my angling obsession some 34 years on.

Bass Fishing in the USA

Bass fishing in the USA always appears a soulless pursuit on cable TV. The fishing looks easy and there seems to be little artistry in playing the poor fish. The anglers bully the bass onto the boat and sling them unceremoniously into the hold. For someone brought up on the genteel Jack Hargreaves' *Out of Town*, it jars.

But back in the day, when satellite telly was but a twinkle in Rupert Murdoch's eye, I found myself invited to a day's bass fishing with an American called Rick. A civil rights lawyer, Rick specialised in defending death row cases. He had a stellar career. On that day, however, work was left firmly back at the office.

Rick's generosity was limitless and he put on a memorable day's fishing. Leaving Columbus way before daybreak, we drove north through the endless golden wheat fields of Ohio, which gleamed as the sun beat down upon them, to meet up with a man called Butch. Now, Butch was a real character. He and Brad, his young assistant, were keen to have some fun. And Butch was the owner of a huge fishing boat on the southern shore of Lake Eyrie, a boat stocked with a ton of night crawlers – lob worms to you and me – and more *Budweiser* than was entirely necessary.

We cracked open the first can of *Bud* as Butch pushed forward the boat's throttle and headed off across the lake. An hour in and the fishing commenced. The tackle was basic: *Abu* closed faced reels and light spinning rods; *Flying C* lures whose hooks were adorned with decent sized night crawlers. The technique was equally basic: cast; retrieve; strike; land; repeat. The rods were bent double all afternoon. The Americans were whacking into good fish and hauling them aboard. We were catching walleye and bass. In my mind's eye, it was a fish a cast.

As we drifted across the water border into Canada – in the middle of Lake Eyrie, on a blazingly hot day, no land in sight, great fishing and endless beers – life could hardly have been better. I caught a decent number of fish – at least one sizeable bass of mine was declared a specimen by Butch – but the Americans were far more prolific. I played my fish at a leisurely pace, while my hosts dragged them in as if they were in the final hour of the *Bassmaster Classic*.

The more we caught, the more we drank. It was a hoot! Even as we headed home, we were hooking fish on our trawling lines whilst supping beers. Brad cooked fresh bass for our supper as Butch steered us to shore. I ended up toppling into the lake as I tried to tie the boat up to the jetty. We could hardly talk for laughing. It was that type of day.

An Angling Adventure to Remember

Venue:

Day: Date: Time:

Water conditions:

Weather conditions:

Catch details:

Fishing method:

Specimen details:

Notes:

An Angling Adventure to Remember

Venue:

Day: Date: Time:

Water conditions:

Weather conditions:

Catch details:

Fishing method:

Specimen details:

Notes:

The Dangerous Edge

Robert Browning once wrote that, "Our interest's on the dangerous edge of things". It might explain the thrill of bass fishing at the end of the rocks off Hope Gap on the Sussex coast.

If the mid-summer tide was right, my mate Sherlock and I would race away from work of an evening and head to the top of the South Downs just outside Seaford. We would walk the mile or so to Hope Gap, take in the view, and then climb down the steps onto the beach. The tide had to be out but on the turn. If we arrived at about 6 pm, we would have an hour or so to collect the bait, traverse the slippery rocks, find a perch above a soon-to-be-filled pool and tackle up, leaving us two hours to fish, as the bass came snuffling in the rocks to feed.

Collecting bait involved prodding and poking around the shallow pools, amidst the seaweed and the shale. All crab-life is revealed. The most entertaining are the velvet swimmers, who never flee, but stick around, claws up, ready for a scrap. The prize bait is a *peeler*, a crab whose old shell has been shed but whose new shell has yet to harden. Fish love them. Half-a-dozen and you are set for the evening's fishing.

Baiting up involves hooking the crab right through its body, but then using thin elastic thread to bind the crab to the hook. Without the binding, the peelers are so soft they come away from the hook when you cast. Replete with peelers, you face the challenge of the diciest 200 yard walk imaginable. Falling hard upon the spiky rocks is grim, like landing on a bed of razor blades. Cuts and grazes are inevitable.

Eventually you find yourself set ready for an intense, exhilarating session. With the sun setting to your right, the sea swirling beneath you and the ever growing swell forcing you back towards the shore, you fish and retreat, fish and retreat, fish and retreat. Ten minutes fishing a deepish pool is good, before you move backwards to the next one. They fill quickly, once the tide gathers momentum. To maximise your fishing time, the trick is to leave it late before you shift yourself. Fear of being swept away competes with the anticipation of a rod-whacking take.

The sunset from out there on the Hope Gap rocks is sublime. The light comes from behind the chalk cliffs and the lower the sun falls, the richer crimson red its rays grow. In the dusk light, reunited back on shore, Sherlock and I would compare catches. Those occasional summer evenings back in the mid-'80s, on the edge of England, were special, not for what we caught but for just the sense of having been there, for the adventure, for the sheer endeavour of it all.

Canny Carp

The Post Office pond was at the bottom of a cow field. To get to it you had to sneak past a huge herd of heifers, which were not always pleased to see you. It was surrounded by trees that cast the pond in shadow, even on the sunniest of days.

Way before the farmer had ever dreamed of selling out to the developers, it was a water where you could spend many a happy summer's evening stalking carp. The pond was home to some decent-sized fish. The biggest I ever caught just made double-figures. You could move from peg to peg, either float fishing bread flake or crusting on the top.

It was lightly fished, but that did not mean that tempting the carp to take your bait was easy. Far from it. One corner at the deeper end was almost overgrown. It was a cattle drink, where the cows came to sate their thirst. The overhanging trees made it difficult to fish. The hoof marks muddied the terrain into the water, up to where the bank dropped off sharply. It was a deep pool that the cows shared with the carp. It was clearly a place where the fish could feed confidently, safe in the knowledge that they would not be disturbed by anglers.

One evening it seemed that every carp in the water had congregated there. I stole along to the corner and – with half a loaf, a 12 foot carp rod, a size 4 hook direct to 8lb line – was determined to see what I could catch. What was, just seconds earlier, a swirling mass of feeding carp became the personification of stillness the moment I arrived.

Undeterred, I baited up. It was impossible to cast. A solid bit of crust, with the hook pushed through and then twisted 180° to set it securely, was dropped directly below the rod tip. I placed and replaced it several times, without having to renew the crust. After about 10 minutes it had become saturated; I dropped it in once more and it sank below the surface. I waited for it to bob back up. Nothing. I twitched the rod tip to check it hadn't fallen off. Without warning, a powerful fish bolted. With no drag set on the reel, the line snapped instantly. *Bang and gone!*

Horsted Place sat on the hill above the pond and overlooked a vast expanse of unspoilt Sussex farmland, of which the pond was an integral part. In the late 1980s, as the golf course building boom exploded across the country, a visionary developer envisaged how he could transform these acres of green and pleasant land into a world class golf course. And so he did. The Post Office pond is now a water hazard in front of the 10th green on the West Course at the *East Sussex National Golf Resort.*

An Angling Adventure to Remember

Venue:

Day: Date: Time:

Water conditions:

Weather conditions:

Catch details:

Fishing method:

Specimen details:

Notes:

An Angling Adventure to Remember

Venue:

Day: Date: Time:

Water conditions:

Weather conditions:

Catch details:

Fishing method:

Specimen details:

Notes:

The Quiet Ones

Mullet are hard to catch. They are the quiet ones – aloof, timid fish. My mate Sherlock and I once fished for them on the tidal stretch of the Ouse just outside Lewes. Typical estuary: water always on the move; grey, ugly mud at low tide; full to the brim at high.

The best time to fish for mullet is as the tide comes in and the fish move up the river, feeding. We spent an hour digging for ragworm to use as bait as the water began to work up between our boots. As the river level rose and we float fished on the bottom, there was a sudden change of atmosphere. The odd silver flash through the green-blue water made the estuary suddenly feel alive. First, Sherlock was into a fish. The mullet fought like a chub, staying deep with a constant, forceful resistance. With Sherlock's specimen barely in the net, I hooked a decent fish. Sherlock caught another, almost immediately. And then nothing the rest of the session. They had arrived, fed, and vanished, all within five minutes.

My next encounter with mullet came in Bude. The first night of the holiday, along the riverside high street, Olly, our mates Mike and James Fitzgerald, and I joined a throng of onlookers marvelling at the shoals of mullet in the estuary. From bridge to bridge there was shoal after shoal, so many that they merged into one super shoal. In just a foot of water. I had the primal urge to begin fishing immediately.

The next day, we were walking through the town and the fish were out in force again. And the following day. And the one after that. Mike reckoned we should buy some kit and get mulleting. I warned him they were hard to catch, but his comments only fuelled my desire to fish.

The provocation was too much. With a birthday coming up the following week, I was in the *North Cornwall Fishing Tackle Shop* before you could say, "fool's errand", purchasing the full kit. The bloke who served me even gave me some advice... "Don't strike too quickly. Mouths are soft. Let it run with your bread." One thing was bugging me, however: despite it being holiday season, I had not seen one person fishing in the estuary. Not one.

I warned Mike as we walked over the canal bridge towards the high street that they might be hard to catch, but that some freelined bread flake might just do the trick. We walked from bridge to bridge and all the mullet – the gorgeous 3 or 4 pounders that had fed ferociously beneath the estuary wall to entertain the crowds – had vanished. It was like the mullet *Marie Celeste*!

No wonder the fish's nickname is the "grey ghost".

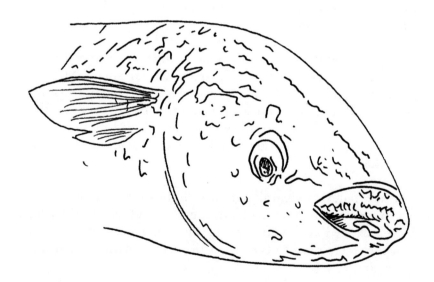

Back to Basics

There is something deeply reassuring about a holiday in the UK. The lack of airport stress, wearing shorts for the week whatever the weather, allowing time to slow down almost to a stop – all these things make holidaying on home shores surprisingly refreshing. I find I can heal better after a tough term of work holed up in Plockton or Abersoch or St Ives.

Pottering about, finding pleasure in the simplest things, soothes the brain, and there is nothing simpler than catching crabs. What is it about crabbing that makes it so damned addictive?! Is it the fact that you can often see crabs take the bait? Or perhaps it is the scariness of the clawed combatants? It might be the thrill of landing one, after so many have dropped off just as you swing them in? Or maybe it is a combination of all those things?

I have always loved taking the boys to catch crabs. Every Easter, in Plockton, up on the banks of Loch Carron, we have caught crabs for nearly two decades. It is a ritual. Our sons are in their twenties now, but one afternoon during the week's stay they will grab a bucket, a couple of lines and a rasher of bacon, and entertain themselves for hours catching crabs off the pontoons in the village harbour. It is important. Our modern, frenetic lives are built around regular milestones in our annual cycle that help us feel rooted and secure, and tempting Scottish crabs with the whiff of smoked bacon is one such moment for our family.

Crabbing with the kids began in Abersoch in 1998. Our Joe was only two. We were holidaying with our close friends the Brown family at the popular Welsh coast resort. We were moving from Sussex to Yorkshire and I was enjoying a summer between jobs, when, for a few weeks, work pressure was minimised. Lloyd and Ali's daughters Rebecca and Kate are just a little older than our

Joe. In photographs from the holiday, we look just like our parents in shots of them from the 1960s.

In those days Rebecca called me "Ladders" because I had lent Lloyd some once. Having been a teacher for 32 years, I have been called worse things. And one afternoon we went crabbing in Abersoch harbour. Rebecca had dressed up for the occasion. Full make-up and glitzy plastic jewellery, including dangly ruby earrings, topped off with a sizeable tiara. *Well, why wouldn't you?*

And we caught a bucket full of crabs. We really could not fail. It was a perfect example of an afternoon having fun, doing very little. When we got back to the house, Ali enquired as to who had caught most, and Rebecca replied, without missing a beat, "Ladders did. He's a *proper* fisherman." I am not sure I have ever felt prouder.

An Angling Adventure to Remember

Venue:

Day: Date: Time:

Water conditions:

Weather conditions:

Catch details:

Fishing method:

Specimen details:

Notes:

An Angling Adventure to Remember

Venue:

Day: Date: Time:

Water conditions:

Weather conditions:

Catch details:

Fishing method:

Specimen details:

Notes:

Addiction

I have valued experiences over possessions for a long time now. People come to realise that material *things* really do not matter at different times in their lives. I reached that moment when I was relatively young. I suppose growing up in a family where it was all we could do to make ends meet explains why I have never really worried about accumulating *stuff*.

Shopping is not a hobby. Something inside me shrivels up and dies if I have to visit the local designer outlet. So, when it comes to my birthday, my wife faces the enduring question: What do you buy the person who has everything? Or, more precisely, what do you buy the person who doesn't *want* any *thing*.

I all but gave up fishing for a couple of years in my mid-teens when I attempted to become a golf professional, but took it up again in my 20s, focusing upon coarse fishing whilst enjoying the odd foray on the sea. Then, in my early 30s, my wife bought me a full day fly-fishing lesson with Bill, an assistant at the Arnfield fishery, near Glossop in Derbyshire. Because I had fished before and had a decent grasp of what to do, I picked it up quite quickly. That said, I spent the first hour fruitlessly thrashing the rod back and forth; the more effort I made the more often the fly line curled down feebly, just beyond the boat's prow. Bill was a patient expert. He talked about rhythm and timing. He demonstrated how to cast effortlessly.

I do love being a learner, especially when the teacher is as good as Bill; always listen and don't be shy to ask for advice. He knew we would catch on a black gnat pattern fished on the surface. I was briefed on the merit of *Gink* to keep the dry fly afloat. In time, I managed to cast a decent enough distance. The black gnat was visible amidst the cut on the water. I thought it was like watching a float, or a piece of bread crust. Without warning, a swirl. The line ran out and I struck like I was trying to drive the hook home into the bony mouth of a double figure pike. Nothing. Bill mentored me gently: "No need to strike, just lift up and away from the fish. Do that and the hook will be set." So that is what I did. Three hefty rainbows later, I was addicted to game fishing.

A day's fishing is the best of birthday treats. The Covid-19 pandemic has helped people realise that a world built on capitalism – which depends upon people purchasing *stuff* they do not need – is not a sustainable model. Many people now know that they can survive quite nicely without visiting the shops. And a silver lining to the pandemic cloud has been a huge spike in fishing licence purchases. Long may it continue.

Rhythm

Ever watched a top batsman push through a forward defensive with minimal effort and then looked on bemused as the cricket ball hurtles towards the boundary? It's called timing. And closely related to timing in sport is a sense of rhythm.

I learnt early on in my golfing career that thrashing at the ball would only propel it forward a few yards, usually in the wrong direction. My dad used to quip that, "*effortless* plays golf" and he was right. When Tony Jacklin led the 1970 US Open at Hazeltine, Minnesota, he went to his locker as he prepared for the final round and found there a note from his friend Tom Weiskopf, which said, simply, "Tempo". He went on to win by seven shots.

When it comes to learning how to cast a fly line as a novice, it is worth remembering a couple of things which will help prevent the line coiling in a floppy pile at your feet; firstly, keep your wrist stiff; secondly, your arm should move sharply from 10 o' clock to 1 o'clock. Beyond those two key tips, all else is rhythm-timing-tempo. When you whip the line back to 1 o'clock for the first time, wait for it to pull against the rod tip behind your head before you thrust your arm forward to 10 o'clock, and then wait until the line pulls again: back-wait-forward-wait-back-wait-forward-wait. You pause until you feel the pull. You always have longer than you think.

When you're casting well, it will, like my dad said of the golf swing, feel *effortless*. The fruit of a perfectly timed cast comes on your final 10 o'clock forward stroke. The fly line should snap against the reel which, in turn, fully extends the leader line forward until, finally, the dry fly lands on the surface of the water as naturally as the real fly it imitates. Which makes it sound all so simple, but even the expert fly fisher fires out a mis-timed cast occasionally.

For months after I had been taught the rudiments of casting a fly line by Bill, I failed more than I succeeded in landing the dry fly lightly on the lake. Until one cast, which, two decades on, I can still see vividly in my mind's eye. I was in a boat on Arnfield and not much was going on. It was early evening and there was little cut on the water. It did not bode well. Suddenly, a decent fish rose 50 feet away. I stripped in my line and rehearsed the "o'clock" mantra in my head. I caught the rhythm of the cast, in a cocoon of concentration. The fly line jolted against the reel, the leader unfurled in slow motion and the imitation fly dropped softly onto the reservoir's surface. It remained there for just a nano-second before the fish took it.

An Angling Adventure to Remember

Venue:

Day: Date: Time:

Water conditions:

Weather conditions:

Catch details:

Fishing method:

Specimen details:

Notes:

An Angling Adventure to Remember

Venue:

Day: Date: Time:

Water conditions:

Weather conditions:

Catch details:

Fishing method:

Specimen details:

Notes:

The Doubters

Yorkshire river fishing is hard to beat. On the last weekend of June a bunch of us go walking in the Dales on our annual *Gentlemen's Walking Weekend*. We often stay at the *Falcon Inn*, Arncliffe. It is as untouched a pub as one can imagine, with Timothy Taylor's *Landlord* poured into white ceramic jugs straight out of the barrel and a gong to declare that dinner is served.

Wonderfully, *Falcon* residents have rights to fish the River Skifare. For countless years I stood atop the main pool in the hamlet and cast my fly line whilst my mates harangued me from the bridge. It is a perfect setting and I never once hooked a fish, much to my companions' amusement. One year, however, with the *Falcon* fully booked, we stayed at the *New Inn*, Appletreewick. And for a fiver you could fish a stretch of the Wharfe.

A sleepless, stuffy night saw me rise at 5 am. I let myself out of the pub's back door and set off across the fields to fish. The whole place felt just perfect. On the far bank the river passed a huge oak tree then widened out into a large pool which converged on a much narrower stretch of the river which ran into a deep trench. I sat on the bank and watched. Trout were rising at the far end of the pool. Not huge, but decent enough. And there was abundant fly life.

I tied a yellow mayfly onto a 2lb leader and dabbed *Gink* onto the wings, fanning them out between my thumb and forefinger. I cast up into the flow on the far side of the river. The fly sat up perfectly, hook below the water line, wings spread above. As it neared the becalmed end of the pool there was an imperceptible movement on the water. The fly had disappeared but I was unsure what had happened.

I kept watching and computing what I'd seen. Of course, there'd been a take. I lifted the rod firmly and, sure enough, the tip dipped over. The familiar, persistent head-shaking struggle of a wild brown trout came pulsing down the line. Its fight was entertaining but ultimately futile. An utterly beautiful 10oz fish had finally broken my *Gentlemen's Walking Weekend* duck. In the blur of the 5 o' clock rise, I had forgotten my mobile, so I could not take a picture of my prize catch. No matter. I was elated.

When I got back to the *New Inn*, it was time for breakfast. Over a Full English, I regaled my mates with a dramatic account of catching a wild brown trout on a perfect Yorkshire dawn. Without the photographic proof, however, they voted unanimously that it was all fabrication. Even to this day, I have yet to catch a fish on the *Gentlemen's Walking Weekend*. Officially.

Hooked Up!

School assemblies can be tedious affairs. All too often teachers stand in front of students and pontificate sanctimoniously about some moral example they have set in their own lives and how students should emulate them in theirs. Alternatively, teachers talk about something that interests the adults amongst the captive audience but which students find fascination-free. I am a particularly good exponent of the latter.

Why I thought our students would be remotely bothered about the art of fly casting, I do not know. But it did not deter me from booking a whole week of September assemblies for a full fly casting live demo. Yes, *you read it right*. I had decided that students would watch attentively whilst I demonstrated to them how to cast a fly. In the school hall. Three hundred students, and their tutors.

On the Monday morning I was in early to practise. On the stage I put a stool upon which I placed an empty plastic water bottle. There was less space than I had anticipated. A cavernous hall felt more like our front room. It was all a bit tricky. But with some improvisation I was soon knocking the bottle off the stool with a well-aimed cast.

An hour later the hall felt even smaller, rammed full of students. I began with the history of the most famous rod makers, *Hardy's of Alnwick* – of some interest to an audience of male pensioners from the North East, perhaps, but maybe not to your average 13 year old.

When it came to the demo, I had to get the first five rows to duck down. It was quite ridiculous. I could see my colleagues looking perplexed. *What IS the head up to?* The students were baffled. They had clearly never seen anything like this masquerading as an assembly before. At least they were paying attention. The bright yellow fly line fizzed through the air. My first attempt thumped against the stage wall. The second went wide. The third wobbled the plastic bottle. There were *oohs* and *aahs* from my audience.

I was enjoying my self-indulgence, confident that the bottle would soon be flying off its perch. I raised the rod again and the line arced above the students' heads. I launched my arm out towards the stage and the rod jolted out of my hand. It took me several seconds to compute what had happened.

The rod was hanging above the parquet floor, dangling next to me. The students giggled. My colleagues looked away. The hall lighting is suspended from the ceiling on a frame of scaffolding poles. The fly line had wrapped itself around one of the poles so securely, it took two caretakers and a ladder to retrieve it at break time. For the rest of the week's assemblies I explained how to learn from your mistakes.

An Angling Adventure to Remember

Venue:

Day: Date: Time:

Water conditions:

Weather conditions:

Catch details:

Fishing method:

Specimen details:

Notes:

An Angling Adventure to Remember

Venue:

Day: Date: Time:

Water conditions:

Weather conditions:

Catch details:

Fishing method:

Specimen details:

Notes:

Observant

It was 7 am and low hanging cloud engulfed the Peak District hills surrounding the Arnfield Fishery. I was fly-fishing for trout, anchored in the middle of the reservoir. There were fish rising all around. I was certain I would catch and that this would be the day we'd have trout for lunch at my in-laws'.

I began with a black gnat fly followed by an olive dun. I swiftly moved on to a mayfly, then a daddy-longlegs. I even was reduced to stripping a bright orange lure through the iron-hued water. Nothing. The fish ignored my several offerings as they continued to tail walk in front of me, waving with their fins. If one had jumped into the boat of its own accord, I wouldn't have been surprised. Cast after cast after cast. An hour later, having worked really hard, I was fishless.

These are the best of times and the worst of times when you are fishing. The last thing you want is for it to be too easy to catch; there has to be some challenge or there is no pleasure when you eventually land a fish. On the other hand, blanking is not much fun.

After a fruitless sixty minutes, I knew something had to change. It was pointless carrying on in the same vein. I was on the verge of returning home having seen a lot of fish but not quite tempting one onto the hook. I took stock of what was happening. My technique was fine. I was casting well; on the final forward cast the line was yanking against the reel so that the leader flew straight out and the fly presented naturally on the water. I had cast in every direction around the boat. I had experimented with a range of different flies. I was using *Gink* to keep the fly afloat. What else could I do?

It was at that moment, reflecting upon what I was doing and what I knew about fish, that I peered over the side of the boat. So miniscule they were almost imperceptible, I could see dozens of green aphids. I had nothing quite so small in my fly box, but I did have a green fly to which I took my scissors and cut away from the hook all but the merest flick of green feather. I tied the fly with a modicum of renewed hope.

Still the fish were rising as I cast for the umpteenth time that morning. My shorn imitation greenfly had sat on the surface of the water for no more than a second before a hefty rainbow trout snuffled it away. I caught three fish in three casts, six in ten. Then the sun broke through the early morning cloud and the trout sank into deeper water.

Vintage

When I set off for the *Murton Car Boot Sale* one morning in March with my son Joe and his three mates, I never thought it would engender a fishing obsession.

A rite of passage for any self-respecting northern teenager is to go to the *Leeds Festival* on GCSE examination results day. We now open school at 8 am on the third Thursday in August, just so that our students can grab their results slips on their way to Bramham Park for four days of debauchery. Whether you're wearing the right braids in your hair is so much more important than worrying if you got a grade B in one *Ology* or another.

We were off to the car boot because the boys needed to raise some money for their *Leeds Fest* tickets. I had a boot crammed full of ostensibly worthless tat that the boys spent all morning trying to sell. The whole car boot thing amuses me immensely. I love it and what I love most is the haggling. That morning we had a boxed up, unused set of kitchen scales on our table. They were marked up at 50p. A bloke enquired as to the price and on hearing the extortionate sum we were charging, put them back down. An hour later the same bloke came round to look at them again and asked if the price had changed; they were 50p *and still he wanted to haggle!*

I left the boys at one point and went rooting about. Joe had said there was a stand in the covered section that was selling fishing kit. There, amongst a whole range of rods, was a tatty looking split cane number. It was way past its prime. When I asked, I was told it would cost a tenner for it to be mine. I left it. But for the rest of the morning it stayed with me.

Authentic old school is what I am, essentially, and after I had told Joe about the split cane rod, he persuaded me to go back.

My ability to strike a deal was no better than the kitchen scales haggler. I swapped a brown spot for a rod of similar hue. I bought *Paul Duffield's Vintage Fishing Rod Restoration Guide* on *Amazon* and began work on my purchase. It was oddly satisfying to strip it back to the bare cane and build it up again, whipping on the new guides, applying the layers of varnish, wire woolling the cork.

Looking at it now, years and many rod restorations later, that first attempt was pretty dire. But I've developed my skills and now I have a couple of once decrepit *Hardy* rods which, whilst not quite looking like new, are in very decent nick. And first time out with that original restoration, I caught a 3lb rainbow on a black gnat off the top.

An Angling Adventure to Remember

Venue:

Day: Date: Time:

Water conditions:

Weather conditions:

Catch details:

Fishing method:

Specimen details:

Notes:

An Angling Adventure to Remember

Venue:

Day: Date: Time:

Water conditions:

Weather conditions:

Catch details:

Fishing method:

Specimen details:

Notes:

Intruders

Seamus Heaney once wrote that, as a writer, you will suddenly 'hear something in another writer's sounds that flows in through your ear and enters the echo-chamber of your head and delights your whole nervous system in such a way that your reaction will be, "*Ah, I wish I had said that, in that particular way.*" This other writer, in fact, has spoken something essential to you, something you recognise instinctively as a true sounding of aspects of yourself and your experience.'

And so it was when I read *Fly Fishing* written by Viscount Grey of Fallodon. At one point in his seminal book, he describes what it feels like to be out in the Highlands, at one with your surroundings… "There are times when I have stood still for joy of it all, on the way through the wild freedom of a Highland moor, and felt the wind, and looked upon the mountains and water and light and sky, till I felt conscious only of the strength of a mighty current of life, which swept away all consciousness of self, and made me a part of all that I beheld."

One Easter we holidayed with our great friends, the Davies family, up in Ullapool. I snuck my fly-fishing kit in the bottom of our packed car boot. My dear mate Huw loves an outdoor adventure. Over an evening glass of *Lagavulin* he proposed an early morning walk around Stac Pollaidh; I suggested we combine it with a dabble on the River Polly. And so we set off, into the clear light of a sharp April day, with the ever-present threat of a downpour.

Recent heavy rain had left the river high but fishable. Casting into eddied corners, I was figure-of-eight retrieving a single hook *Silver Stoat's Tail* bought especially for the occasion, with scant success. I was immersed in the moment when Huw nudged me in the back. I turned to find a magnificent stag staring at us. Stac Pollaidh stood imperiously in the background, framed by the animal's antlers. My fingers stopped moving. With the sun shining down from behind, the silhouetted stag appeared dark, splendid and at home. Imposters in his world, Huw and I dared not speak. Its Medusa-style stare had left us petrified.

Viscount Grey's words ghosted the moment. It might have been one minute or ten, but in its own time, this most Scottish of beasts took its leave of two insignificant Englishmen. Feeling both at once diminished and enhanced, we realised we could move again. With wordless glances, we acknowledged the wonder of what we had witnessed. I stripped in my line and, breeze behind, cast way upstream. A fish rose for the fly as it dropped onto the water and, my mind elsewhere, I missed the only take of the day.

Ultimate

Long, steaming hot June days mean one thing and one thing only to the ardent fly fisher, and that is a late mayfly hatch. There is no point being on the river until 8.30 pm as the fish will only feed frenziedly for the last two hours of the day.

And so it was a couple of years ago, when I set off for the Rye with half-a-dozen brand new mayfly patterns, an old *Allcock's* reel, and a beautiful, 90 year old *E Kerry of Lockton* split cane fly rod. To this day, it is still my best split cane restoration job. I bought if for £30 on *eBay* and took six months to restore it to its splendid best. It is slightly soft, but casts well and is undeviatingly straight.

Moving upstream from Ryton Bridge I could see a great deal of fly activity. The specific mayfly pattern which best matched the hatch was a simple *Olive-Grey Dun*. I sat observing a long straight stretch of river and settled upon a sizeable fish that was gorging itself on mayfly. I squatted down behind a bankside bush and cast twenty yards upstream. With a relatively light, unweighted line, casting is demanding. But when you get it right and the line snaps against the reel, the fly lands so gently that it barely breaks the surface tension of the water.

I began fishing well after nine o'clock. It was still wonderfully warm. My target fish was feeding voraciously. It was, however, ignoring my offering. Every time I cast, the water went quiet. When I stopped casting and watched, the fish rose repeatedly.

Giving up is not an option so I kept on casting as the minutes ticked by and the sun dropped inexorably lower in the sky. The thing is, doing the same thing and expecting a different result is a sign of madness. But I didn't have any other option. My mayfly choice was spot on and I was casting well into the slight breeze. I was below the bankline and obscured from the fish's sight by the undergrowth.

Then, suddenly, I had a stroke of luck. I cast and a split second before my fly landed, the fish rose to take a mayfly. My fly landed an inch or two beyond the rise and, in a moment of unguarded spontaneity, the fish took mine too. I struck and knew the hook was set. I fell backwards, but kept stripping the line in as the fish swam downstream towards me.

The fight was furious but the *Kerry* split cane rod performed perfectly, cushioning the surging runs. Five minutes later, I was photographing a 4lb 8oz chub caught off the top on a summer's evening, next to the vintage split cane rod I had renovated. It doesn't get much better than that.

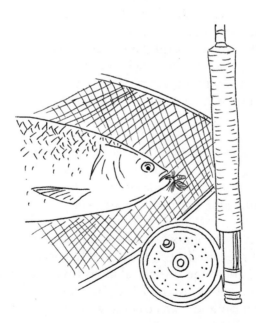

An Angling Adventure to Remember

Venue:

Day: Date: Time:

Water conditions:

Weather conditions:

Catch details:

Fishing method:

Specimen details:

Notes:

An Angling Adventure to Remember

Venue:

Day: Date: Time:

Water conditions:

Weather conditions:

Catch details:

Fishing method:

Specimen details:

Notes:

Violating Zeno

Most of the fishing I have ever done has been on naturally formed lakes, ponds and rivers; waters that have taken eons to form. The stream at the bottom of the field, Abbey's Lake, The Yorkshire Esk, The English Channel, The Pacific Ocean – all natural habitats for wild fish.

Ironically, where I learnt to fly fish, Arnfield Reservoir, is a man-made water in Longdendale, North Derbyshire. It was constructed in 1854 as part of the water system that serves urban areas of Greater Manchester. It has proven a happy hunting ground for me over the past two decades. I have caught many a decent rainbow on that water, as well as a number of brownies. I have no reason to be critical of Arnfield, but one session left me feeling dismal and clarified for me why I fish where I fish.

When I visit Arnfield I tend to hire a boat. I eschew the motor engine for the oars, exploiting the opportunity to exercise fishing whilst I fish. There is something splendid about being anchored in the heart of this reservoir. The views are remarkable: to the west is Manchester; the south looks over to Glossop with the Snake Pass beyond; east is the Woodhead Pass and the Pennines; and northwards you'll find Saddleworth Moor. Steve, who runs the fishery, is a fine host and keeps everything in decent nick.

There is nothing not to like about Arnfield. But this particularly day something died inside for me. I had been fishing hard all morning. I had zig-zagged about, changing both fly and location. I missed a tentative take off the top on a black gnat over in the far corner but, apart from that, the fish seemed either disinterested or down deep. A chilly north-west wind was driving down the reservoir.

I was heading for the car park corner, rowing past the anchored boats near the lodge, when Steve, who was making his way to the end of the jetty, asked what I'd caught. When he learned I was fishless, he suggested that I slap my fly line on the surface of the water in front of the jetty. He explained that the splashing tricks the fish into thinking it is him throwing them feed pellets. The stockies love it, he told me, as do many of the anglers who frequent Arnfield. Such fakery, apparently, saves blanking.

I felt obliged to do what he suggested, whilst he looked on, expectantly. I whisked my fly line back and forth on the water. Within a few seconds there was movement on the top as the rainbows came in search of food. I ended up catching four fish, all the same size, about 1¼lb, the weight of a freshly stocked trout. Steve beamed and sauntered back to the lodge, happy to have helped. He had no idea that I felt like I had sinned against Zeno, the Patron Saint of Anglers.

Motivation

We hadn't lived in York long when we took our four year old son Joe fishing. I think I had some romantic notion that if he started young he would be hooked forever, so to speak. There are many well-stocked fishing venues in the York area. Some are significant waters, others are not much more than puddles.

We took Joe one Sunday afternoon up the A19 to Tollerton Ponds. It looked like we would catch – all the testimonials sounded positive and the weather was warm and sunny. All we needed was a place where he would get a bite a cast and land a few small rudd, roach and perch. We weren't asking much.

There are three ponds at Tollerton and we chose to fish the one nearest the road. It is a tight little spot and there was nowhere near the space required for both of us and Joe. We were hard against the road, on a tiny platform amongst the reeds, with a fence hemming us in. Somehow, we managed to get set up with a light float and a size 16 hook. At that point I felt astrologically predestined to catch.

Joe tried to cast but met with meagre success. He just could not time the release and the float dropped at his feet again and again and again. Snag followed snag. And as soon as we eventually got the rig out in the swim and the rod settled, he was in amongst the maggots. One thing I had not anticipated was Joe's fascination with everything else bar what was happening to his float. He spent the whole time gazing at all the magical things around him – the road, the birds, the farm buildings, the floats, the landing net. Most of all he was interested in the maggots.

He had seen the swirling mass of multi-coloured fly larvae when I had prised open the lid of the box for some hook bait. Big mistake. Half the maggots were in the water before we knew it. I did my utmost to keep calm. I did not want to spoil things by barking at him. Louise turned away for laughing. Joe thought the maggots were just the best thing. He began throwing them in one by one to watch them swim. I missed a bite. Louise walked away.

It was a carnival of chaos. I promised my son all sorts of treats if he were merely to sit down for five minutes and *blinking well fish!* I had more chance of being made head of the Roman Catholic church than Joe doing what I asked of him. *Why would he at his age?* Louise took him for an adventure walk around the pond. Had we come fishing for him or for me? I suspected the latter, if truth be told.

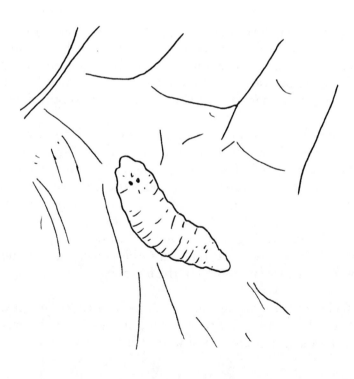

An Angling Adventure to Remember

Venue:

Day: Date: Time:

Water conditions:

Weather conditions:

Catch details:

Fishing method:

Specimen details:

Notes:

An Angling Adventure to Remember

Venue:

Day: Date: Time:

Water conditions:

Weather conditions:

Catch details:

Fishing method:

Specimen details:

Notes:

Fun in the Sun

Holidaying in Greece is a blast! For several years in a row, a number of families in our friendship group stayed in the same villa complex on Skiathos, a small Greek island, east of the mainland. What I adore more than anything about such holidays is the wall-to-wall 90° sunshine and cloudless, azure skies.

The noisy air conditioning and too many *Mythos* beers always mean I am awake before dawn, and what better thing to do on a cool warm morning than to go fishing off the rocks in the centre of Skiathos town? I take a handline and fish with bread flake legered on a size 14 hook. It is mindless fun. My mate Will came once and caught a couple of tiny rainbow wrasse and a superb two banded sea bream. The latter must have weighed all of 3oz, but to us, skipping about in the rising sun's rays, it was a specimen.

I often wonder why fishing whilst on a Mediterranean holiday is such a pleasure. The weather is the main factor, for sure, but spending time doing something inconsequential and utterly fun makes you feel like a boy again. On the last morning of that particularly holiday, I went to Agia Paraskevi beach with another mate, Nick. We had three hours to catch a mullet.

Two days earlier, I had been tracking a couple of terrapins in the narrow streams which feed into the sea when I'd spotted a shoal of small silver fish. They looked like chub. The thought of them had gnawed away at me. On the final morning, I could resist that urge to go fishing no longer. I managed to persuade Nick to come with me. He had never fished in his life. I briefed him. We HAD to catch one and the noon deadline added an edge to the whole escapade.

The fish were only accessible through ten foot tall reeds. We had to sling the handline with the bread-baited hook blind over a wall of brambles. We missed bite after bite. It was stinkingly hot. I was scratched and sweaty. Nick was melting. The clock was ticking. As I got more obsessed, Nick got more excited. A fish fell off half way up the bank. Another missed bite. The bait was running out. We crashed about the undergrowth as the fish swam up and down the stream.

With minutes before we *really* had to go, a four-inch long mullet came flying over the bushes like the *Silver Surfer*. Nick grabbed it, lost it, grabbed it, lost it. Finally, I snatched at it but it slipped clear of my sweaty fingers and dived back into the water. A final act of utter buffoonery, which left us no less jubilant at having caught our quarry with seconds to spare.

Pike

Big pike are awesome fish in the true sense of the word. Male pike rarely go beyond 10lb. The monsters with preternaturally large, barbed-wire mouths are all female. During their spawning season, from December to March, river pike seek out still water to conserve energy as they swell with strength-sapping roe.

Where the River Derwent sweeps round and joins its counterpart, the Rye, just north of Malton in deepest North Yorkshire, the confluence creates a large triangle of relatively quiet water. It is the perfect spot for huge, hungry pike to congregate during the winter months as the rivers flood. Perhaps four times a season, my mate Tom and I would trek across the recently flooded fields and pit ourselves against the sharp-toothed rulers of the riverbed.

For a decade or more, Tom and I enjoyed tremendous sport fishing the "Triangle". We came to understand where the fish would lay and what best attracted their attention. Over time, several mates joined us.

Bob, using a small, seemingly insignificant, blue toby lure, landed a pike too big for Tom's 30lb maximum scales. I once brought along my mate Nick. When we arrived, I told him to cast to the far bank and retrieve the lure slowly. I wanted a coffee and declared that I was only going to tackle up once he had caught a fish. Within four revolutions of the reel handle, he was into a double-figure pike. I hadn't even had time to unscrew my flask. Another close friend Tim, a seasoned angler, quietly informed me that the 15 pounder he caught there was a lifetime personal best fish.

Despite the seeming inevitability of catching pike at the "Triangle", there were times we blanked when we were certain conditions were perfect and others, with the river running too high and mud-coloured, when we couldn't fail. Our best session saw us catch a 14 pounder, two 16 pounders, a 19 pounder and one just over 26 pounds. All in two hours. And I lost the biggest: a fish that I couldn't shift off the bottom of the river. Before it threw the hook, all I could do was walk up and down the bank following it, as though I was taking a surly bullmastiff dog for a walk.

The thrill of the take when a pike hammers into your lure, steams away across the pool and then tail walks before succumbing to the net with a rueful grin is hard to beat. Suddenly, that experience became all too rare at the "Triangle". One winter went by quietly and then another, with just a single fish broaching the double figure mark. At the fag end of that second sparse season, I discovered two reasons for the decline as I watched a pair of ravenous otters catch and then, on the far bank, devour a sizeable pike.

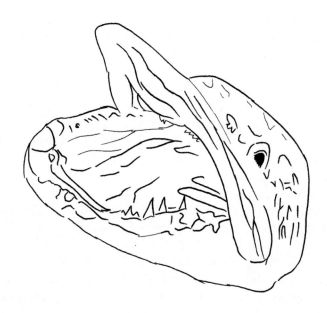

An Angling Adventure to Remember

Venue:

Day: Date: Time:

Water conditions:

Weather conditions:

Catch details:

Fishing method:

Specimen details:

Notes:

An Angling Adventure to Remember

Venue:

Day: Date: Time:

Water conditions:

Weather conditions:

Catch details:

Fishing method:

Specimen details:

Notes:

Hope

The Yorkshire Esk saw very few fish during the long, dry summer of 2018. It was a delight, then, on yet another fishless day to come upon Adrian Blant's splendid sea trout. This was no ordinary sea trout; Adrian's was a carving in a huge name block at *Rake Cottage* in Glaisdale. Over the space of three weeks, I saw the carving develop, from pencil sketch to the finished work of art. And what I admired about Adrian was his attention to detail. When he talked about his work, he pointed out the three features of his carving which differentiated it from a salmon: the eye position, the tail and the spots below the lateral line.

Adrian is an expert in every sense. A born and bred Yorskshireman and self-taught sculptor, his work takes him far and wide. The previous year he had spent several weeks in America, plying his craft. This was his first stone fish and he was keen to carve one or two more. Certainly, when I can afford to retire and buy the riverside country cottage of my dreams, I fully intend to have one of Adrian Blant's sandstone creations adorning the front lawn.

That stone sea trout was the only one I saw that entire summer, despite the endless Saturdays and Sundays I spent in search of a real life version on the River Esk. On the very last day of 2018 Tom and I returned to the pike "Triangle" where the Rye meets the Derwent. It was a bleak afternoon, and reminded me of Thomas Hardy's poem, "The Darkling Thrush". Hardy, on the final day of the 19th century braves the day-long, deep frost and ventures out on a walk. He can find nothing to give him hope. Just as his despondence begins to deepen, he hears a thrush, "in blast-beruffled plume" begin to sing and in the bird's "carolings" wonders whether there is "Some blessed Hope, whereof he knew/ And I was unaware." It is a poem which has always resonated with me.

Anglers never lose hope. There is always the promise of a fish, *if you have just one more cast.* Whilst it was a fun way to end the year – I always enjoy an outing with Tom – the days of huge pike seemed a thing of the past. I was using a blue plug, whipping it through the water pretty sharpish. With the last, casual cast of the session, as the final light of the year slid away, I whacked into a decent enough fish. Suddenly, it was thrashing around, leaping out of the water.

There was no pike-style tail walking across the river's surface, however; the flashes were silver, not green and gold. Making one hell of a fuss was a decent sized sea trout. The fish was in beautiful condition on its 60-mile trip back to the North Sea. It was a spawn-free kelt, my symbol of Hope as the New Year was ready to dawn.

Alone

Fishing is therapeutic. It calms the heart and salves the soul. To get away from the world when "I'm weary of considerations, And life is too much like a pathless wood" – as the American poet Robert Frost wrote in his wonderful poem "Birches" – I will grab my rod and some basic kit and take myself off to a river bank.

And so it was one winter's day, when I was under horrible pressure at work and the house was full, that I thought it time I tried out my recently renovated *Gamages of London* six foot long split cane spinning rod. At least a decade older than me, it was the real thing, with a lustrous yacht varnish finish on the cane, near perfect cork handle, and the original porcelain guides. Antique split cane rods are vulnerable things. They can appear stunning, whilst inside the cane has rotted to dust. The best test of a split caner is to push the rod tip into your front room ceiling at home and bend it double. If its core is decayed, you will soon know as your head is showered in splinters.

The Rye was swollen but the river level was falling. The sediment was settling and I thought it possible that a fish would be able to see a large red and white, deep-diving plug, if I could drag it past its snout. That said, I wasn't bothered about catching. It was just good to be out. I fished hard, covering the swim systematically. Back and forth, back and forth. The rhythm of the afternoon wore on. I lost myself in the unthinking nature of the task.

The relentless casting and recasting helped me clarify the challenges facing me at work until I could park them in a mental metal box and strap the lid down. My arms ached with the effort. Back and forth, back and forth. The rod was straining just with the demands of retrieving the lure against the formidable current.

I cast again, right across to the far bank, and reeled swiftly to get the lure down to the riverbed and thought for a second I had snagged on the bottom. It was not the usual take of a pike. As I exerted some force the *snag* began to move across the river. There was nothing spectacular about the fight. It was a grim battle as a decent fish resisted my pressure with the help of the swollen river's flow. As the rod bent double I thought there was something about it that seemed ever so slightly odd.

I kept the strain on and just as the fish rolled into the net, the top length of cane snapped at the ferrule. I was left with a magnificent 12lb pike, a clear mind, and the task of stripping down my *Gamages* spinning rod for spares.

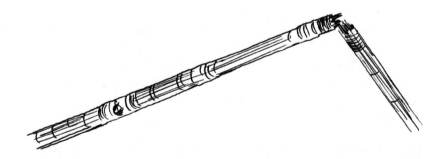

An Angling Adventure to Remember

Venue:

Day: Date: Time:

Water conditions:

Weather conditions:

Catch details:

Fishing method:

Specimen details:

Notes:

An Angling Adventure to Remember

Venue:

Day: Date: Time:

Water conditions:

Weather conditions:

Catch details:

Fishing method:

Specimen details:

Notes:

Plockton

Loch Achaidh na h-Inich. It is difficult to pronounce but beautiful to behold. The Loch in question is a wonderful water a few miles south east of Plockton up in the Scottish Highlands.

We found Plockton by chance a couple of decades ago and now visit every Easter. It is a place where we go as a whole family. Our mates, the Davieses, holiday with us and we all agree that it is the most precious time of the year. We spend a week taking all day, every day, to do very little. And it is easy to live the simple life in Plockton, where to be content requires not much at all. I have never thought that retiring abroad, or to somewhere new in the UK, made any sense. Why devote decades to building a life in a specific location you call your home and, just when you have more time on your hands to spend with your mates, retire to somewhere where you know no-one?

Now, however, I think I could while away the final phase of my life in *Plockers*. We have been so many times, we feel it is our second home. Some fishing kit, a bottle of decent single malt and the promise of dinner in the *Plockton Inn* is all you need for a perfect day. And when we are on holiday up there, I will always slink away one afternoon, drive over the hill and fish *Loch Achaidh na h-Inich*, just because I can.

There is a tiny, accessible corner of the loch for fishing where I try my luck, year-in, year-out, with light fly gear. The water is iron-brown, the result of its peaty surroundings. The key ingredient of *Lagavulin* 16 year old, which gives its smoky finish is the same thing that makes the depths of this Highland Loch so dark.

I dream of taking a wild Scottish trout off the top, but that dream has never been realised. One mild early spring afternoon, however, I was day-dreamingly casting and retrieving a *Fulling Mill Orange Nugget* lure, stripping it in, casting out, covering the water systematically in front of me – from 10 o' clock round to 2 o' clock and back to 10 o' clock – when there was a swirl just beyond my lure. I cast again. Nothing.

The next cast I began retrieving the moment the line hit the water. The take came almost immediately. It was a modest fish but didn't feel like my longed for trout. It sped off. There was none of the wriggling struggle of a brownie. Rather, the early surges were short lived and the fish came to the net with few histrionics. It was a perfectly formed jack pike of about a pound. It was an incredibly dark green, almost black. A *Lagavulin* pike, for sure.

Brief Encounter

My youngest son has the propensity to be an angler. That said, every time I ask him to come fishing he refuses. My approach goes something like this:

"Olly?"

"What?"

"I've sorted out a real treat for you this weekend!"

"I am NOT going fishing."

So, on one of those non-days between Boxing Day and New Year's Eve, I was as surprised as anyone when he agreed to a quick piking session.

Olly had just begun secondary school. He was a young 12 year old. I think he came fishing that day just to be kind to his poor old dad, in the spirit of Christmas. We drove to Ryton Bridge on the Rye. The low cloud did not prevent it being finger-numbingly cold. The previous week's substantial flood was receding, the water was coloured but clearing – in other words, conditions were perfect for catching pike.

I reckoned a heavy, bright yellow jelly lure lobbed out to the far bank and drawn back slowly along the bottom of the swirling pool just below the bridge would do the trick. I explained this to Olly. His first cast fell limply into the water under his feet. His second, however, plonked into the far eddy. I helped him with the rhythm of the retrieve and as the yellow jelly came up just a few feet out, a prehistoric beast lunged at the lure, missed and swirled back into the depths. "I'm scared dad," said Olly.

I persuaded him to cast again. On his second retrieve he complained he was stuck on the bottom. I grabbed the rod above the handle and yanked it hard into the air. The drag on the reel zinged out. "You're in Ol!" I yelled and talked him through how to play the fish. It was an explosive two minutes. Pike fight like they hunt, in high-energy, intense bursts. When they see the bank they surge away, often tail walking spectacularly as Olly's did, but once done, they will surrender and drift into the landing net.

It took me both hands and a huge effort to haul the pike up the bank. It was magnificent – its deep green and bright gold flanks were blemish free. It banged my 14lb scales straight down. I estimated it was at least an 18 pounder. Olly was stunned. I managed to get him to cast again. Nothing. He wanted to go home, content that he'd caught and made me happy.

I eked one last cast out of him. Three retrieves in and another thumping take had the drag screeching again. It was a 12 pounder to add to his impressive opener. Olly had launched five casts and caught thirty pounds of pike. We left for home just 15 minutes after we'd arrived.

The bewildering thing is, I'm not at all sure he's been fishing with me since.

An Angling Adventure to Remember

Venue:

Day: Date: Time:

Water conditions:

Weather conditions:

Catch details:

Fishing method:

Specimen details:

Notes:

An Angling Adventure to Remember

Venue:

Day: Date: Time:

Water conditions:

Weather conditions:

Catch details:

Fishing method:

Specimen details:

Notes:

You Should be in Skye

We have spent the best part of two decades visiting the Isle of Skye and not once have we seen an otter. The area is famous for otters, for goodness' sake – Gavin Maxwell's *Ring of Bright Water*, the sentimental, heart-breaking tale of his otter Mijbil, is set on Skye! But have we seen an otter? *Have we hell as like!*

The first year we holidayed in the Highlands with the Davieses, we took our five young boys to see the otters. The *Glenelg to Kylerhea Ferry* is one of the smallest and scariest ferries you are ever likely to find. It brings you onto Skye at the *Kylerhea Otter Hide*, where you can sit and watch the otters. Allegedly. The otters certainly *hide* there, that's for sure.

We didn't see one on that first day on Skye and we have never seen one since. Our theory is that when the Easter holidays arrive, the Highland otters know we are due to visit so they get a National Coach down to the River Rye in North Yorkshire to avoid us. One year we got back from Skye on a Saturday and I went fishing for pike on the Rye the next day. The first thing I saw after I parked my car at Howe Bridge and walked 50 yards down the riverbank? Yes, of course, a damned otter!

In fact, I have seen a few on the Rye, which is both good and bad. Good because it means the fish stock is plentiful, otherwise the otters would not be so abundant, and bad, because, as my earlier "Pike" tale tells, they are devouring the fish.

Once, when Will and I were fifty yards from our "Triangle" pike hot spot, we stopped and for a full five minutes watched a huge, quite stunning otter, two rod lengths from where we stood, rise and dive, rise and dive as it helped itself to as many chub and dace as it could eat. Witnessing such a remarkable display of gracefulness first-hand, reminded me that the word "otter" derives from the Anglo-Saxon word for water – as though animal and element are one and the same thing.

The most breath-taking otter spot was with Tom. We had been at the "Triangle" but a few minutes. In fact, I was still setting up. It was a morning of crisp coldness; ice was forming across the guides on Tom's rod. I had my back to him, side on to the river. He whispered my name. There, about three feet away in the water, *literally* under Tom's rod, was an otter. We stayed rooted. It hung in the water, taking deep breaths. Its nostrils flared. We could hear it snorting. It arched its back and looked straight at us. Spooked, the otter tipped up upon itself and was gone, with swirling, aquatic panache.

Catching a Sea Trout

One fruitless cast, slightly short of perfect, is followed by another where the lure flirts with the overhanging branches at the pool end and then sinks out of sight before the slow, deliberate retrieve begins, and then a knock and then, a nanosecond later, a whacking thump and the spectacle begins as my brain computes what is happening, as the moment I have anticipated since dawn, a dozen hours earlier, arrives, but still, when it happens, my senses are scrambled by the shock of it and my arms and hands fumble to establish control of the rod and reel which are near ripped from my grasp as the fish understands, more acutely than me, that the fight is on and summons all the energy it possesses as it makes for the depths, lunging downwards to the river bed as I resist its frantic dash, striking hard, setting the treble hooks, rod arching towards the river, the reel's drag screeching, though no sooner I think I know where it's gone than it changes tack and surfaces, skittering across the pool and I marvel for an instant at its wild, thrashing, tail-walking, gymnastic frenzy, then, before I realise it, the fish plummets down and down only to turn tail and hurtle skywards at a rattling rate, emerging from the water in a fleeting leap for freedom, an awesome, ephemeral display of powerful, piscine aerobatics which ends abruptly when it dives again, lurching one way then the other and I'm scanning this way and that for where it will appear next and suddenly it's just a few yards away, surging into the river's edge, seeking sanctuary amongst the tree roots, and my pumping heart tells me this is the decisive moment, this is when I can lose it all, where the fish swaps itself for something gnarled and immovable, and the gamble begins because not enough force and it's lost in the roots, too much and the hooks rip from its jaw, so I hold my nerve, pressing my elbow that little bit harder on the rod butt, tightening the line, increasing the strain, ramping up the pressure and for those crucial seconds the dipping, plunging rod tip telegraphs down the line the news that we're still connected, the hooks are secure and now the balance of power shifts as I ease the fish, slowly, back into the current and the struggle resumes as it dives again for the riverbed, but this time I'm in control when, without warning, the rod bend eases and suddenly I see the silver broadside ripple across the water as it surrenders, the lure securely hooked through its jaw, the resistance waning, and then it's under my boots and in the net, hoisted high above the river's flow, trophy-like, a three pound sea trout –

An Angling Adventure to Remember

Venue:

Day: Date: Time:

Water conditions:

Weather conditions:

Catch details:

Fishing method:

Specimen details:

Notes:

An Angling Adventure to Remember

Venue:

Day: Date: Time:

Water conditions:

Weather conditions:

Catch details:

Fishing method:

Specimen details:

Notes:

Sealed

In Brighton we could see the sea from our bedroom window. There was something elemental and reassuring about having a waterway within view. When we moved to York, we gravitated towards the river and, for what now seems like a real steal, bought a house that literally faces the Yorkshire Ouse on New Walk.

In the flood of 2000, when the river was 5.5 metres above its normal levels, the river appeared for a week in our front garden. But the worry of being flooded every so often does not outweigh the sheer joy of being able to pop out for a quick fish at 5 am in the summer months. I have a spinning rod permanently set up in the back yard from June to October. I have caught decent enough pike, perch and chub over the years, but the one species that has eluded me is the salmon.

Downstream, three miles from York city centre, is Naburn Lock and, for a while, a £5 day ticket gave you access to a stretch of river below the lock which was rammed full with salmon. Come early April, after a dry March, you'll find the migratory fish caught below the lock in low water. They get up to the waterfall, find they cannot progress until a spate, and sit there getting increasingly irritated. If you're a better angler than me, you'll drag a *Flying* C across a Naburn salmon's nose and provoke it to lunge for your lure. I have seen Tony the bailiff catch specimens up to 20lbs.

The best time to begin fishing is five hours after high tide at Albert Dock in Hull. As the water comes up from the East Riding, so do the fish. I stood there once, early morning, and counted 24 salmon jumping in front of me. It was like an air show with fish spiralling out of the water in a metaphorical two-fingered aerial display of contempt for me and my inadequate angling skills. On the way back to the car that morning I stopped at the lock and filmed the scene. A minute's footage saw several fish hurtling out of the water.

It really shouldn't be so hard to catch. One morning seemed perfect. The weather was temperate, and during the walk down from the lock to a sandy-bottomed spot where the fish rest up, I had seen and heard fish crashing about the water. I tackled up, excited and distracted every few seconds by the sound of salmon plunging around. I stood ready to cast for the first time but realised I had company. There, across the river, directly in front of me, was a huge, self-satisfied looking seal who proceeded to haunt the swim all session and nullify what slim chance I had of breaking my duck. I still haven't hooked a salmon.

Heron

Just to my left a trout, no more than four inches long, hurled itself out of the shallow water.

I had been fishing just outside Danby village deep in the North Yorkshire Moors. I am not sure there is a place on this planet where I feel as content as I do when I stand on the bank of the Yorkshire Esk, spellbound by the prospect of catching a wild brown trout. There is nothing quite like it.

I began the session at the Beggar's Bridge. I then worked my way along the wooded stretch of the Esk at Rake's Common and finally fished the winding stretch towards Danby upstream from Duck Bridge. I took three rods: fly, float and spinner. I found success on each one.

At Rake's I caught a perfectly formed small wild brownie on a dry fly. I had seen the trout rise several times; the moment my black gnat hit the river's surface the fish obligingly rose to take it. It was one of the day's many highlights.

Wild brown trout live their lives in streams and rivers. They are fine, slimline predators and sparklingly beautiful. From the preternaturally large, coal black eye, the tapered array of innumerable black spots gives way to a carefully arranged pattern of a dozen or so red counterparts. The gills emit a mother of pearl shine. The dappled grey flanks merge into a creamy underbelly. And the red adipose fin is a sure sign that the trout is a wild brown.

By the time I had plonked myself down amongst the meadow grass to fish a small but inviting pool, I had landed more than a dozen wild brownies. They fight hard, no matter how miniscule, wriggling intensely. When they are spent, they will lay across your hand in all their aesthetic glory.

My float was dancing about indeterminately when the trout jumped. The fish's belly-flop re-entry made a larger sound than one might have expected. It was enough to attract my attention. A heart-beat later, from upstream and around the corner, I heard two airy wafts followed by a much bigger splash. A heron appeared fleetingly before stepping into the cover of an overhanging tree, directly opposite where the leaping four-inch brownie landed.

I kept watching. It wasn't long before the heron began tip-toeing towards its quarry, a picture of predatory elegance. Four steps in, it stopped. Its amber eye caught mine. For the briefest moment it could not compute what it saw. Its stare dolly-zoomed towards me until it was inches away from my face. We were locked together, eyeball to eyeball, beak to nose, bound by the pursuit of the same prey. I held the bird's glare. The river flowed on. And then the heron beat its broad, grey wings and was gone.

An Angling Adventure to Remember

Venue:

Day: Date: Time:

Water conditions:

Weather conditions:

Catch details:

Fishing method:

Specimen details:

Notes:

An Angling Adventure to Remember

Venue:

Day: Date: Time:

Water conditions:

Weather conditions:

Catch details:

Fishing method:

Specimen details:

Notes:

Depth Charges

Every year we lose an hour in the springtime and gain an hour in the autumn. Both changes of the clocks are important markers in the annual cycle. Losing an hour in March is the clarion call for game anglers to renew their fly lines; gaining an hour in October heralds the winter pike season.

One of the joys of gaining an hour in the autumn is that the last week of October, just before the salmon and sea trout season finishes, is blessed with lighter mornings. It is also half-term. The summer of 2017 was a wet one and in October the fish were moving up the Yorkshire Esk in their droves. It had been a long half-term at work and I was tired. Nevertheless, on the last day of the holiday I set off for Glaisdale at 4.15 am. I figured I would be fishing at Beggar's Bridge by 5.30 am. And I wanted to be the first on the river.

The drive through the early Sunday morning gloom seemed interminably long. I first began to doubt myself when I emerged from Rosedale up on to the peak of the moor and, instead of the glow of a rising sun, there was a wall of darkness. I came down into Glaisdale and parked up. It was pitch black. I could get a single bar of 4G on my mobile and eventually discovered that the sun was due to rise at 6.49 am. Even with the clock change, I was over an hour early. Fool.

As I leant against my car boot, I heard a short fizzing noise, followed by a crashing splash, as though someone had thrown a boulder off the bridge into the river. And then another. *Fizzzzzzzz-*nano second pause-*crashhhhhhhhh!* I realised it was fish jumping. I walked up on to Beggar's and the *fizz-pause-crash* routine was repeated every minute or two. It was as if the sea trout and salmon knew I was there and were treating me to an airborne display they knew I would never see.

133

I returned to my car but there was still no hint of the darkness lifting. I stood there listening to my quarry revelling in the river just a few yards away. Time ticked on and I eventually tackled up. I stood in the river as the sun rose, working the water with my *Black Fury* lure, and still the fish were leaping, celebrating the end of the fishing season. I fished all day. I covered the whole stretch of the Esk, from Glaisdale to Castleton, via Lealholm and Danby.

As the sun began to set and the afternoon drew to an early close, my final cast of the day produced a fresh, silver flanked sea trout. It made my ill-timed start worth every wasted minute.

Priest

Mother said, quite casually, "Go and check if the hamster is OK. I haven't heard it squeaking for a few days". The hamster was kept in a large cage, formed from the brick base of a long-gone greenhouse and covered by chicken wire. At mother's command I went to check upon our hamster's wellbeing. Sure enough, there it was, on its back, claws pointing skyward, stiff with rigor-mortis. I was a tad confused.

"Mum", I said, "it's out there lying on its back, pretending to be dead".

At the age of five, my first confrontation with death was perplexing. I knew the hamster was dead, but thought it couldn't *actually* be dead. But next to go was Sammy the cat, from cancer. Then Sammy the cat's replacement – also called Sammy – from an argument with a car, followed by the next cat's kittens which my dad took a spade to and buried in the garden. We found a dead fox and my brother chopped off its flea-ridden tail and brought it home as a trophy.

Then I killed a trout I caught in the stream below our house with a stick. By the age of eight my innocence was lost forever.

My primary school mate Ben and I brought home a chub which his mum cooked for tea. It was utterly inedible, chock full with bones. To kill a coarse fish, we learned, was a distasteful act of barbarism. When you game fish, however, whether to take home your catch is always a quandary. A sea trout, bright silver, fresh from its salt water home, will taste delicious, cooked in butter with a little light seasoning. Even stocked rainbow trout from a Peak District reservoir, with its peaty water, are delicious on the barbeque.

I find that the bigger the fish, the more difficult it is to deliver the final blow – *the last rites* – with my Priest. As well as being a great angler, Tom shoots deer. He skins them in the field where they fall. But even Tom, hardened countryman of Danish-Polish descent, found that he lost the stomach for deer hunting for several years. For a while he couldn't quite pull the trigger and fell such a magnificent beast.

I caught a beautiful Esk sea trout once. It gave a superb fight, tail-walking, hurtling this way and that. It eventually came to the net and was suddenly illuminated, in all its splendour, by the late afternoon light through the canopy of trees. It could not have looked more magnificent. I scrambled up the bank, unhooked it and laid it out on the thick meadow grass. I gazed at it. It weighed about 4lb, fresh as you like. I didn't have to kill it. We both knew I'd caught it. I could it return it to the water, no harm done. I reached for my tackle bag...

An Angling Adventure to Remember

Venue:

Day: Date: Time:

Water conditions:

Weather conditions:

Catch details:

Fishing method:

Specimen details:

Notes:

An Angling Adventure to Remember

Venue:

Day: Date: Time:

Water conditions:

Weather conditions:

Catch details:

Fishing method:

Specimen details:

Notes:

Indian Ocean Antics

The two week holiday to China, and then a week to recover on Bali, cost a small fortune. When we got married in 1988 we had bought a one-bedroomed flat, so small it was like an inverse Tardis. It was actually smaller than it looked when you stepped inside. But four years later, we decided to spend all our savings on a summer holiday, rather than upgrade to a house.

And so we found ourselves discussing the range of excursions available on Bali with the tour rep over a morning coffee on the terrace of the *Sanur Beach Hotel*. As I scanned the list of trips, one caught my eye: *Tuna Fishing*. The Badung Strait separated our shoreline from Nusa Penida Island and for an indecent number of Indonesian Rupiah you could spend the morning catching fish I had only ever eaten out of a tin.

Two days later, I was squatting on a traditional wooden fishing boat, heading out into the Indian Ocean. The boat was no more than four feet wide and 30 feet long, with a single sail for propulsion. It had huge wooden frames either side which sat on the surface of the sea to provide ballast and prevent the boat from sinking immediately in the ocean swell.

Two people fishing, and two expert crew; the latter skipped about the boat like they were traversing the wall bars in a school gym. I was, frankly, terrified. One of the crew stood on the edge of the boat as lookout. He would yell and point at where he had seen fish leaping, and his mate would manoeuvre the sail and head off after them.

Squatting down in the boat, I couldn't see anything but huge walls of water. At the stern was a seat from which you fished; I was ushered into it and given a pre-cast hand line. Within seconds there was an unceremonious whack on the line and the crewman gestured for me to crank the line in. A 3lb Tuna was soon flipping about in the bottom of the boat. Next thing I knew I had caught a four-foot long barracuda, which took some landing. It caused significant excitement amongst our Balinese hosts.

And that was me done. I swapped places with a Chinese bloke and resumed clinging on to my rickety seat. I thought I was going to die. Before I knew it, the boat was heading back to shore. On the beach we were photographed with our catch before it was divvied up between the crew, who were delighted at the prospect of selling the fish to the local hotel. I, on the other hand, was just glad to be alive.

Yet I had fished on the Indian Ocean and caught tuna and barracuda. And I'd lived to tell the tale. That's all anyone really needed to know.

Disorganised Chaos

I cannot recall whose idea it was to suspend the school timetable for an activities day, but I saw it as a golden opportunity to run a fishing trip. This was no ordinary fishing trip, however, this was an outing to a well-stocked coarse fishery for my small group of 14 year olds who followed the Certificate of Personal Effectiveness (COPE) course instead of a GCSE.

If you think back to your school days, instantly forgettable lesson after instantly forgettable lesson must have floated by because it is very difficult to recall any but a mere handful. The ones you can recollect are the ones in which an extraordinary event occurred, usually involving a moment of particularly poor student behaviour and an especially traumatised teacher.

What you do remember, however, beyond the occasional lesson, are the school trips, the sporting events, the annual musicals. That is why I generally give in when a member of staff asks if we can have an activities day.

So, along with Gev, one of our wonderful teaching assistants, ten students and I set off in a minibus, packed with as much borrowed kit as I could muster, for a sunny afternoon's fishing. No one on board had fished before, bar me and a lad who was a highly proficient angler. It was fascinating to see his behaviour transformed; usually one of the most disruptive characters in school, he was suddenly the epitome of responsibility. He clearly felt valued as the senior member of the group and behaved accordingly. He went on to catch tench and carp all afternoon. His dad came along to watch, much to his obvious delight. His swim was an oasis of calm amidst the storm.

I set up rods and had the students fishing in pairs in five adjacent pegs. It was disorganised chaos. Teaching just one pair how to cast was a challenge, but to keep track of five rods, in the hands of complete beginners, was almost too much. If I'd asked them to get their tackle in a mess on purpose, I'm not sure they would have done a better job than the tangles they were generating by accident. It struck me that, as they mature as anglers, people become increasingly blind to all the tiny checks they make to ensure that their kit is working well. Total novices have yet to learn that unconscious competence of the seasoned angler.

But we caught lots of silvers, everyone notched, Ella got a booter – much to her peers' amusement – and we returned to school a happy bunch. A full decade later, in a local supermarket, I chanced upon one of the intrepid COPE crew stacking shelves. I stopped to have a chat. The first thing she recalled? Our activities day out fishing. *Of course it was!* It had all been worth it. Mission accomplished.

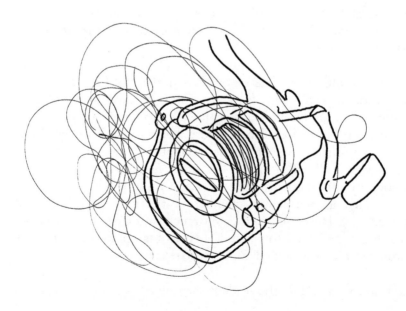

An Angling Adventure to Remember

Venue: ....

Day: .... Date: .... Time: ....

Water conditions: ....

....

Weather conditions: ....

....

Catch details: ....

....

....

....

Fishing method: ....

....

....

....

Specimen details: ....

....

....

....

Notes: ....

....

....

....

....

An Angling Adventure to Remember

Venue:

Day: Date: Time:

Water conditions:

Weather conditions:

Catch details:

Fishing method:

Specimen details:

Notes:

Puncture Bridge

Anglers are great company. They are, on the whole, a gregarious lot. And generous too. People who fish are keen to share their knowledge about a water, what bait they have been catching on, what swims are best, what time of day the quarry feed. It is as though we have a common foe against which we unite.

Not much beats telling fishing tales over a few pints in the pub at the end of a day's fishing. Indeed, actually going fishing is about the only thing that beats talking about fishing! My day job involves running a school in York. It is an all-consuming enterprise. I have over two hundred members of staff to get to know. I like to understand what makes them tick. We are all human beings first and employees second. We all have lives beyond our work that are more important. I go out of my way to engage in conversations with my colleagues about their lives outside of school; it is an essential part of an effective leader's job.

Any head teacher knows how important it is to have great support staff and John Cobb, one of our excellent caretaking team, is up there with the best. When we interviewed him he was concerned that the work pattern would interfere with his passion – pigeon racing. He has since gone on to keep budgerigars. He is also a tremendous angler. He reads a great deal. His knowledge of the history of fishing in our region is second to none. He takes his grandson fishing nearly every weekend. With retirement on the horizon, he is working on his match-fishing skills.

Since I appointed John we have spent many moments sharing our knowledge of the countryside, one of which occurred as I was leaving work one summer evening. He told me about how, when he had crossed the mist-shrouded Yorkshire Ouse early that morning, he has been reminded of his dawn-start fishing trips with his dad

fifty years before. He told me about them in detail, even down to
one of the bridges where his bike always seemed to get a puncture.
His reminiscences were a sonnet waiting to be written...

Fishing Lines
for John

His old man crossed the landing to his room
And, careful not to wake the eldest son,
He whispered to the youngest through the gloom
The needless exhortation, *John, come on.*
The weather's good. And like two guilty thieves
They rode unnoticed through the early dawn;
A getaway on bikes along York's streets
To *Puncture Bridge.* The morning mist adorned
The slow, resplendent Ouse – just like this June,
Fifty years on. Those stolen early starts,
Sat with his dad beneath the fading moon,
Were when he learnt the expert angler's art:
When to *strike*, how to read the river's flow –
Such things that only fishermen can know.

Blank

Teenage rivalry can manifest itself in the least likely circumstances, even when you're fishing for carp.

I first fished Raker Lakes when one of the so-called "lakes" was a trout pool. It was stocked with decently sized rainbows and I managed to wheedle out a couple one damp autumn afternoon. Since 2008, however, all the five lakes just outside Wheldrake, on the edge of the Yorkshire Wolds, have been dedicated to coarse fishing. They are, in essence, muddy puddles, but muddy puddles where it is easy to catch fish.

Taking Olly and his mate James to Raker Lakes for a carp-fest to entertain them on one of those long afternoons in the middle of the summer holidays seemed like a great idea. My good mate Ant – James' dad – came along too. I always find it incredible that any male member of the human species has never been fishing by the age of five, but neither Ant nor James had ever angled before. I love helping others catch. Always happy to play the ghillie, I gain significant satisfaction from other people's joy at hooking and landing fish, especially if it is their inaugural session.

Olly had been to Raker's before and caught a number of carp on crust off the top. He was happy to show his mate how to set up and cast. I helped Ant, who had come straight from work. He was all smart casual – leather-soled shoes, chinos, a sharp shirt – just the garb for fishing. Nevertheless, after about half an hour we were sorted: three rods in three adjacent swims; loose crust out to get the carp feeding; and a growing sense of anticipation.

James had decided to fish for silvers on a float. He was soon getting bites. His instinct was to aim the rod at the float and reel like crazy when he hooked a fish. Olly patiently showed his mate the merits of letting the rod take the strain, even for a 2oz rudd. Four or five fish in, and James was getting the hang of it. Olly, meanwhile, was fishless. Then James hooked and landed a nice mirror carp of a couple of pounds. He was beaming.

And then Ant's crust disappeared in a swirl and he was slipping around trying to hang onto a hard fighting common. He started giggling as the fish tore up and down the swim. I netted Ant's first ever fish, which weighed in at over 5lb. There were photos and high fives and celebrations more akin to scoring a goal at the Stretford End.

Olly just fished on. By the end of the afternoon the novices were novices no longer, having both bagged a decent haul. Olly, however, blanked. And to this day he'll admit just how irritated that made him feel.

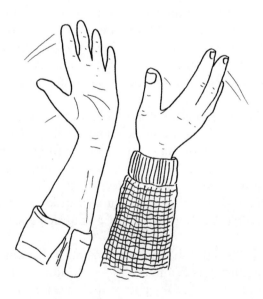

An Angling Adventure to Remember

Venue:

Day: Date: Time:

Water conditions:

Weather conditions:

Catch details:

Fishing method:

Specimen details:

Notes:

An Angling Adventure to Remember

Venue:

Day: Date: Time:

Water conditions:

Weather conditions:

Catch details:

Fishing method:

Specimen details:

Notes:

Mackerel

Most people who fish have caught a mackerel. They are, proverbially, ten-a-penny. In the summer months, they can be caught most anywhere along the British coastline. I remember my dad pointing them out to me on holiday, standing on the beach at Norman's Bay; black storms of swarming fish dotted across the surface of the English Channel.

I caught my first mackerel on Brighton Marina. A full house on a set of six feathers took some retrieving. Sherlock and I brought home a plastic dustbin full of them. Literally. We ran out of room in his freezer and spent an evening delivering fresh fish to our mates across the city.

We are not the mackerel's only predators; they are relentlessly preyed upon. Whilst fishing down on the Marina, I saw a huge bass succumb to a live-baited, free-lined mackerel. When I fished in Cuba for tuna, the boat's skipper followed the mackerel shoals to locate the bigger prize. Some of the best mackerel sport has been had sitting on a harbour wall with light tackle, float fishing small sprats on a size 6 hook. They take fast and fight hard. I've caught them every time I have been sea fishing, without fail, from Brighton to Bali and beyond. And I have caught pike on mackerel fillet in the middle of North Yorkshire, miles from the sea.

On holiday in Cornwall once, we were granted a pass out for a day's fishing, as long as we returned with fresh fish for supper. The five of us got chatting to the bloke in charge of the *Bluefin Charter* boat company stand on St Ives harbour. I love angling chat. Any afternoon, in every town across the land, there are men standing around in fishing tackle shops chatting nonsense. The *Bluefin* bloke was no different. He guaranteed we'd catch fish. *It was a dead cert.* And not just mackerel – red gurnard, whiting, and even bullhuss were a possibility.

We fished two, mile-long drifts about 500 yards off shore. I had listened to the boat hand. He'd suggested jigging the feathers just off the bottom. Sure enough, I had a take almost immediately and a small red gurnard joined the mackerel bucket. Always good to listen to anglers more experienced than yourself. We saw a sunfish float lazily by. Charlie, James, Mike and Olly caught plenty, as did the other six paying customers.

We returned to the harbour with a string of mackerel each to barbeque. As we drove back to our holiday home, I was struck by the splendour of these oft-traduced fish. The sharp sunlight fell upon the mackerels' maze of blues and greens and blacks; they really are quite magnificent creatures. They taste good too.

Whilst they may sit near the bottom of the food chain, we should all, perhaps, give thanks to the humble mackerel.

Common Ground

The last thing students want is for a teacher to think he can be their mate. It is the worst thing. Even if you are a newbie twenty-something teacher, to Year 9 students you are *ancient*. That does not mean, however, that you just turn up and teach them robotically; that does not work, either. To be a good teacher, you have to get on with youngsters.

Good teaching is built upon forging mutually respectful relationships; it is *so* important. When I teach naughty boys – you know, the cheeky, jack-the-lad 14 year olds – I spend lots of time getting to know what they do outside of school. It gives me something to chat about with them during those idle moments when they are queuing at the door waiting for the change of lesson, or when I meet them round school.

I know it's unbelievably obvious, but to build positive relationships with lads, you have to know your sport. The greatest common ground between us is football. I support Manchester United – of course I am a Red, *I was born in Sussex*. When United lost the league to Manchester City at the end of the 2012 season, I walked into the library, Monday period 1, to find the whole class of boys I was teaching standing in front of the newspaper rack pretending to read the centre pages of all the papers. Every light-blue sports back page confronted me in welcome.

Understanding what makes boys tick is a crucial step in creating a productive student-teacher relationship. And, so, when it spreads around the playground that you are into fishing, you find that you have a whole raft of new and different students to chat to when you are on lunch duty.

I once caught a huge, lithe, late springtime pike. I was fishing in relatively shallow water on the Rye with a small, orange *Rapala* lure for trout when this magnificent beast of a fish struck like the proverbial steam train. It was a full ten minutes before the 22 pounder was in the net. My teacher mate Steve took a fab photograph of me cradling it, with its cavernous mouth agape.

I told a number of students the story in dramatic fashion one break time, with suitable embellishments, and said that if they wanted to see the picture of the pike, they were welcome to have a look the next time they came by my office. They absolutely loved it. Now, nipping into the head teacher's office is hardly something naughty lads do at school, but for weeks afterwards, as news spread of this pike I'd caught, knock after knock at my door was followed by the timorous enquiry, "Sir, I've heard you caught a big pike. Just wondered if I could have a look at the photo…"

An Angling Adventure to Remember

Venue:

Day: Date: Time:

Water conditions:

Weather conditions:

Catch details:

Fishing method:

Specimen details:

Notes:

An Angling Adventure to Remember

Venue:

Day: Date: Time:

Water conditions:

Weather conditions:

Catch details:

Fishing method:

Specimen details:

Notes:

Gift

It had been a pretty ordinary day's fishing. Whilst it was running higher than one would have liked, the Rye wasn't in bad shape, and it was a decent colour. Tom and I had escaped the shopping madness of the last Saturday before Christmas and were determined to make the most of a snatched afternoon's fishing.

Tom had pointed out a wild deer, which I'd missed as we drove across the fields towards the "Triangle". Fishing with Tom for the last two decades has been an education; I am a relative city-boy compared to him. We can be driving around the North Yorkshire countryside and he'll spot something I would never have seen. He has a huntsman's eye. Once we were fishing on the Esk and he said, suddenly, "I've got to go. The wind is in the right direction. I have a deer to stalk" and off he went. And the next time we met he regaled me with a tense tale of stalking, shooting and skinning his quarry.

That day, we had caught one double-figure pike each. My biggest ever is 26lb 8oz, but it isn't my specimen catch. Possibly the best measure of a fish is its weight as a percentage of the British rod caught record for the species. My huge pike was a mere 56.6% of the record pike, a monstrous beast of 46lb 13 oz. My greatest ever specimen fish weighed 66% of the record, and I caught it that afternoon.

Time was drifting on, the sun was low in the west and winter darkness was preparing to envelop us. For the last quarter of an hour I presented a small imitation perch jelly lure with a long curly tail. First cast – BANG! Second cast – BANG! Third cast – BANG! Three jack pike on the bounce. They were great fun and suddenly an ordinary session had been transformed into a memorable one.

In the last of the winter sun, I walked upstream to a bankside bush, which, when the river runs high, causes a very slight eddy in the margins beneath your feet. I dropped the curly-tailed lure into the water and jigged it around, just in case there was a fourth small pike resting there, ready to strike.

Within seconds, I was in. But it was not a classic pike attack. I just found the rod arching over and the line moving along the riverbed, straining towards the roots of the bush. The fish worked hard to elude capture. Tom played ghillie and, eventually, he scrambled up the bank with an extraordinarily large chub in his net. It was a truly magnificent creature. The fading light only enhanced its deep-set, silver flanks. It weighed in at 6lb 1oz, two thirds of the biggest chub ever caught in Britain.

To this day, that early Christmas gift remains, arguably, my best ever fish.

Plans

It is always good to get a pass out, to go fishing with a clear conscience.

A chilly Saturday in January. I had checked the River Rye water levels online; the flood was subsiding and after lunch it would be absolutely perfect. An afternoon pike fishing with Tom was nailed on. I just had to make sure I had done all the things on my to-do list. First task was to clean and tidy downstairs. Empty the dishwasher, wash the kitchen floor, wipe down the hob, vacuum the front room and sort out my office. Done.

Next was a visit to the dump. There was a bit of a queue. I tapped the steering wheel in frustration. Eventually, I was given a slot to access the refuse cages to dispatch our rubbish. I stopped at York tackle to buy a pack of imitation pike jelly lures for the afternoon's sport. I nipped up to work to collect some marking – Year 10 essays on *Of Mice and Men* – before heading across the city to *Tesco's*. I filled up the car, bought some kindling wood and coal, found an ink cartridge compatible with our printer and then went to collect the ironing from Mandy.

I got back to the house just before noon, raked out the ash and built a fire. A flask of fresh coffee and I was ready, pass out thoroughly earned. I chucked the tackle in our new *Nissan Quashqai* and made for the countryside.

The thin winter sunlight suffused the landscape and the Yorkshire Wolds appeared Turneresque. As I came over the Huttons Ambo hill and Malton hove into view, my heart skipped a proverbial beat, as did the car's engine. I changed gear and put my foot down on the dual carriageway by-pass, anticipating the fishing; there were further misfires. As I pulled into the lay-by at Howe Bridge, I was mulling over what was wrong with the *Nissan*. I'd only had it a few months. Surely it wasn't going to break down.

As I waited for Tom, I felt increasingly sick. I had always had a petrol motor; this one was diesel. My mind replayed the visit to the garage. I found the fuel receipt in my wallet. *Unleaded*. *Un-bloody*-leaded. All that rushing around to get the pass out and I'd put half a tank of petrol in my diesel car. Tom arrived. Despite his protestations, I insisted he fished – the river looked *perfect*.

I rang the AA only to find that, despite having been a member for over 30 years, they still wanted £299 up front before they would send out the specialist rescue van. The AA man was finishing the paperwork in the fading light when Tom returned, fishless. As some wag once quipped, the easiest way to make God laugh is to tell him your plans.

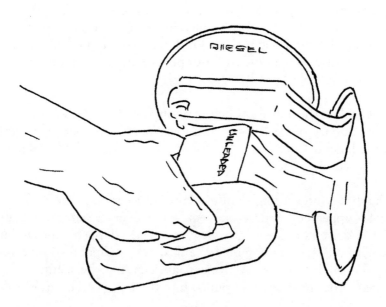

An Angling Adventure to Remember

Venue:

Day: Date: Time:

Water conditions:

Weather conditions:

Catch details:

Fishing method:

Specimen details:

Notes:

An Angling Adventure to Remember

Venue:

Day: Date: Time:

Water conditions:

Weather conditions:

Catch details:

Fishing method:

Specimen details:

Notes:

Gene Pool

The 2020 Coronavirus pandemic was miserable in many ways, but for the first dozen weeks the weather was generally glorious. At the end of May, a hot day was drawing to a close when I set off with an old *Milward's* split cane fly rod in search of a wild brown trout. What made that evening particularly special was my eldest son came along to watch.

When lockdown was announced, Joe had retreated from London where he had been building a life, to live back at home. He'd spent the first eight weeks ensconced in his old bedroom studying for his Masters exams. When I asked him if he fancied coming fishing, I never thought he would, but I was mistaken. He jumped in the car, eager for some late sunshine on his wan cheeks.

Talking to sons can be arduous. Plonk them in a car with you, where you both stare straight ahead without having to look at each other, and they are suddenly garrulous. And so it was with Joe, as we chatted about anything and everything, about his search for a job, his exams, life in the capital, when the pandemic would end, whether we would catch a fish.

We stood on Ryton Bridge looking down onto the Rye. There had been a mayfly hatch. We walked upstream, chatting. We sat and watched the sand martins busy in and out of their nesting holes on the far bank. We talked some more.

And as the sun dropped ever lower in the early summer sky, downstream to our right a fish rose. I alerted Joe and we watched. In silence. Another rise. Two more, in quick succession. A big fly sailed downstream, its struggles emanating radio wave ripples to any lurking predator. It didn't last long.

I signalled to Joe to follow me and we stole down the bank until we were just below the fish. We watched a little longer. The *Milward's* rod zipped the fly out into the breeze, but just short of where the fish was rising. Joe crouched to my left, net ready. A lower cast and the leader line unfurled perfectly to land the mayfly imitation softly on the water, six feet above the fish. Nothing. And again. Nothing.

The sunlight thinned. But just as I was ready to concede defeat, BANG! I lifted the rod and the trout took off gloriously, hurling itself across the river, this way and that. Seconds later Joe stood grinning in front of me, with a decent wild brownie in the net. And we were done. One take, one fish.

As I shut the car boot and we looked back across the fields to where we'd fished, Joe said, "I enjoyed that, dad. We should do it more often."

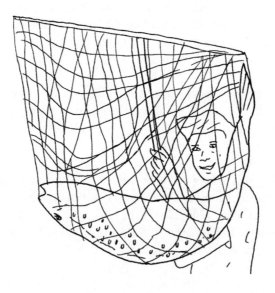